Captivated

CULTIVATING AN INTIMATE RELATIONSHIP WITH GOD

Nonda Houston

GPH®
Gospel Publishing House

Contents

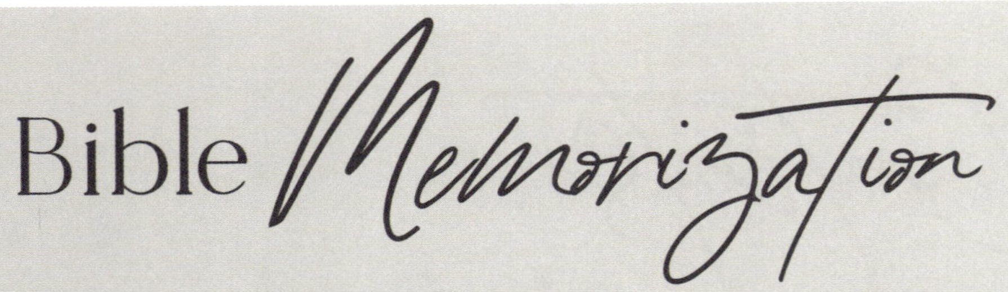

Bible Memorization

Each week throughout this study, a memory verse is provided.

Here are a few facts to know:

- Bible memorization holds great importance and can have a tremendous impact on your discipleship journey. By hiding God's Word in your heart, it enables you to internalize Scripture and deepen your connection with the Lord.

- It's also important to realize that you are in a spiritual battle that is not fought or won in the natural, physical realm.

- Since it is a spiritual battle, you have been given a spiritual weapon. The Bible refers to the Word of God as your sword (Ephesians 6:17; Hebrews 4:12). As you pray the Scriptures, you are aligning your thoughts with God's, dismantling strongholds, and declaring the promises in your life and in your world.

- When your Bible isn't with you, the Word can be hidden in your heart. It is a valuable resource to draw from in times of need providing guidance, comfort, and strength in the face of life's challenges.

- Scripture memorization is a source of wisdom and a reminder of God's promises. It's a powerful source of encouragement and a way of passing along your values to the next generation.

Study *Tips*

1. Get Comfy

PUT ON SOME COMFORTABLE CLOTHES! BEING UNCOMFORTABLE CAN MAKE IT HARDER TO FOCUS.

2. Find Your Space

ESTABLISH WHERE YOU'LL STUDY! FOR SOME THAT'S A COMFY CHAIR OR THE KITCHEN TABLE. FOR OTHERS THAT MIGHT BE AT CHURCH OR AT YOUR FAVORITE COFFEE SHOP!

3. Gather Your Supplies

BE SURE YOU HAVE YOUR BIBLE AND STUDY BOOK! SOME COLORED PENS AND HIGHLIGHTERS CAN BE HELPFUL TOOLS AS WELL!

4. Pour Some Fuel

BIBLE STUDY JUST WOULDN'T BE COMPLETE WITHOUT YOUR FAVORITE DRINK! MY FUEL OF CHOICE IS A WARM VANILLA LATTE OR A CREAMY ICED CHAI! WHAT'S YOURS?

5. Put Away Distractions

TUCK AWAY ANYTHING THAT MIGHT DISTRACT YOU DURING YOUR QUIET TIME SO YOU CAN BE FULLY PRESENT.

6. Prepare Your Heart

PRAY BEFORE YOU BEGIN YOUR STUDY EACH DAY. ASK GOD TO PREPARE YOUR HEART FOR WHAT HE WANTS TO REVEAL TO YOU THROUGH HIS WORD.

introduction

Years ago, I heard the story of a well-known worship leader who had the most profound dream. He saw a picture of angels around the throne of glory, each one bowing down and saying, "Holy, holy, holy." They were in complete and continuous awe of God. Their reverence never ceased, he explained, as each time they looked at God, they saw a new aspect of His character and nature. Truly, His greatness knows no end. While this was only a dream, it has inspired me to realize the vastness of our God and to know Him more. His love is truly captivating.

My friend, God created you and knows you intimately. You have been His idea since before time began. He chose everything about you and then set you in this time and space. You are the apple of your Father's eye, created in the image of God for the purpose of having an intimate relationship with Him.

Over the next six weeks, we will explore our relationship with God and how to know Him more though our emotional, physical, spiritual, relational, and intellectual experiences. The foremost way to learn about God is through the Bible. It is God's love letter to us, revealing His plan of redemption and heart for humanity. This study will dig deep into Scripture as you meet face-to-face with the reflection of your heart. There will be questions, contemplation, and prayer. This is the road to discipleship and the way to know Jesus more.

Like the angels in the dream, we too can live a life in awe of the greatness of God as His character is revealed to us through trials, tests, trauma, and temptation. No matter the outcome, how redemptive it is to know that nothing has been wasted during a season of challenge because we can emerge knowing God more intimately than before.

Some religions have thousands of gods, each with its own defining characteristic. As Christians, we know that the Bible reveals the one true God who is so magnificent that we will never exhaust learning the extent of His greatness, power, and love. How blessed we are to be invited on this grand adventure of knowing Him!

"WHEN GOD HAS DEEPENED US,
THEN HE CAN GIVE US HIS DEEPER TRUTHS,
HIS PROFOUNDEST SECRETS, AND HIS MIGHTIER TRUSTS.
LORD, LEAD ME INTO THE DEPTH OF THY LIFE
AND SAVE ME FROM A SHALLOW EXPERIENCE."[1]

As you open the deep places of your heart to God and seek Him through His Word and prayer, you will be transformed and forever marked by the Holy Spirit. Let the journey begin!

with love,
Nonda Houston

[1] Lettie B. Cowman and James Reimann, *Streams in the Desert* (Grand Rapids, MI: Zondervan, 1996), 270.

WEEK
One

Trust in the LORD
with all your heart,
and lean not on your
own understanding;
in all your ways
acknowledge Him,
and He shall direct
your paths.

Proverbs 3:5–6, NKJV

A Journey
to Knowing
God More

Week 1 | Day 1

A Journey To Knowing God More

Throughout our life, we meet many people along the way—family, friends, people at work, school, church, and your community to name a few. Meeting someone on an airplane or a stranger at the grocery store will typically be a once-in-a-lifetime moment. Some relationships fall into the category of acquaintances, others will grow into friendships, and fewer still will result in lifelong connections.

As close as these relationships can be, none are as intimate as the relationship shared between a husband and wife. Marriage is another level of knowing and being known.

When it comes to knowing God, the same range of relationship exists—from casual acquaintance to a deep connection. The difference in this relationship though is that the level of intimacy we enjoy with God is contingent upon the level of invitation we extend.

Through the decades of my spiritual journey, I have found something that has deepened my relationship with God: the pursuit of knowing Him more by developing an intimate relationship with Him. Proverbs 3:5–6 has been the signature passage of my life that has guided me through many troubled waters.

As we study this Scripture, the verbs in the text reveal our actions steps to reach the desired outcome—God's direction in our life. The first two are to "trust" and "lean not" or depend. The next is perplexing: acknowledge (translated *seek* in other translations). How do we acknowledge God in all our ways?

The word *seek* or *acknowledge* in this verse comes from the Hebrew word *yada*, which also translates as *know*. When we read it this way, it casts new light on how to acknowledge Him. In all our ways, *know* Him by acknowledging who He is in light of our circumstances.

We know we can bring our prayer requests to God. It's good and right to share with the Lord our circumstances and the cries of our heart. But this verse is also an invitation to invite Him into the middle of the mess with us. Telling Him about our problems and knowing that He is in the thick of it with us makes a big difference. For every problem there is a promise, and a name of God whereby He reveals a side of His character that we may not have known before. Our crises become opportunities to know Him experientially, personally, and intimately.

Reflection

Take inventory of your relationship with God.
Where are you right now? Where would you like to be?

____

____

____

____

What do you imagine a closer relationship with Jesus would look like in your life?

____

____

____

____

Prayer

I INVITE YOU, LORD, TO DEEPEN MY RELATIONSHIP WITH YOU.
I WANT TO KNOW MORE ABOUT YOU AND
I WANT TO KNOW YOU MORE.

AMEN.

Getting to Know God

Week 1 | Day 2

Getting To Know God

Have you ever been fortunate enough to watch a bird family in a nest? Inside, a few tiny eggs are nestled in the twigs while the doting parents are ever so busy keeping watch. When the baby birds hatch, the mama bird's activity increases even more. She is tasked with eating for herself and her babes. She is literally eating for two, three, or four, unpleasant as it sounds, so she can regurgitate her food back to them until they are mature enough to leave the nest and fend for themselves. It may be a disgusting illustration, but it vividly portrays the idea of living solely on secondhand spiritual knowledge.

God gave Moses the process by which sinful people could stand before a holy God. Once a year, on the Day of Atonement, the high priest would make a sacrifice before entering the Holy of Holies and sprinkling blood on the mercy seat that rested on the ark of the covenant. Then he would emerge from the Holy Place and place blood on the altar before making another series of sacrifices on behalf of the people (Leviticus 16). But when Jesus hung on the Cross and died giving His life as the ultimate sacrifice, the veil that covered the entrance to the Holy of Hilies was torn supernaturally from the top to the bottom (Matthew 27:51).

Under the old covenant, the priest stood and ministered before the altar day after day, offering the same sacrifices again and again. But our High Priest offered himself to God as a single sacrifice for sins, good for all time. Then He sat down in the place of honor at God's right hand (Hebrews 10:11–12).

This was God's way of saying that Jesus was the new intermediary to get to God. Through Jesus' sacrifice, we have forgiveness of sins and direct access to the Father. This revelation transformed the apostle Paul from a zealot persecuting Christians to the man who said,

As you sit at the feet of Jesus to foster a one-on-one relationship with Him, be honest with Him. Lean into His presence and listen for His voice. God, give us a hunger to seek You and a thirst to know You so that nothing else will satisfy.

Reflection

Am I relying solely on others to feed me spiritually?

____

____

____

____

How can I deepen my one-on-one relationship with Jesus? What apprehensions arise when I think about this?

____

____

____

____

Prayer

*JESUS, FAN THE FLAME OF MY HEART AND SET
MY SOUL ON FIRE FOR YOU.*

AMEN.

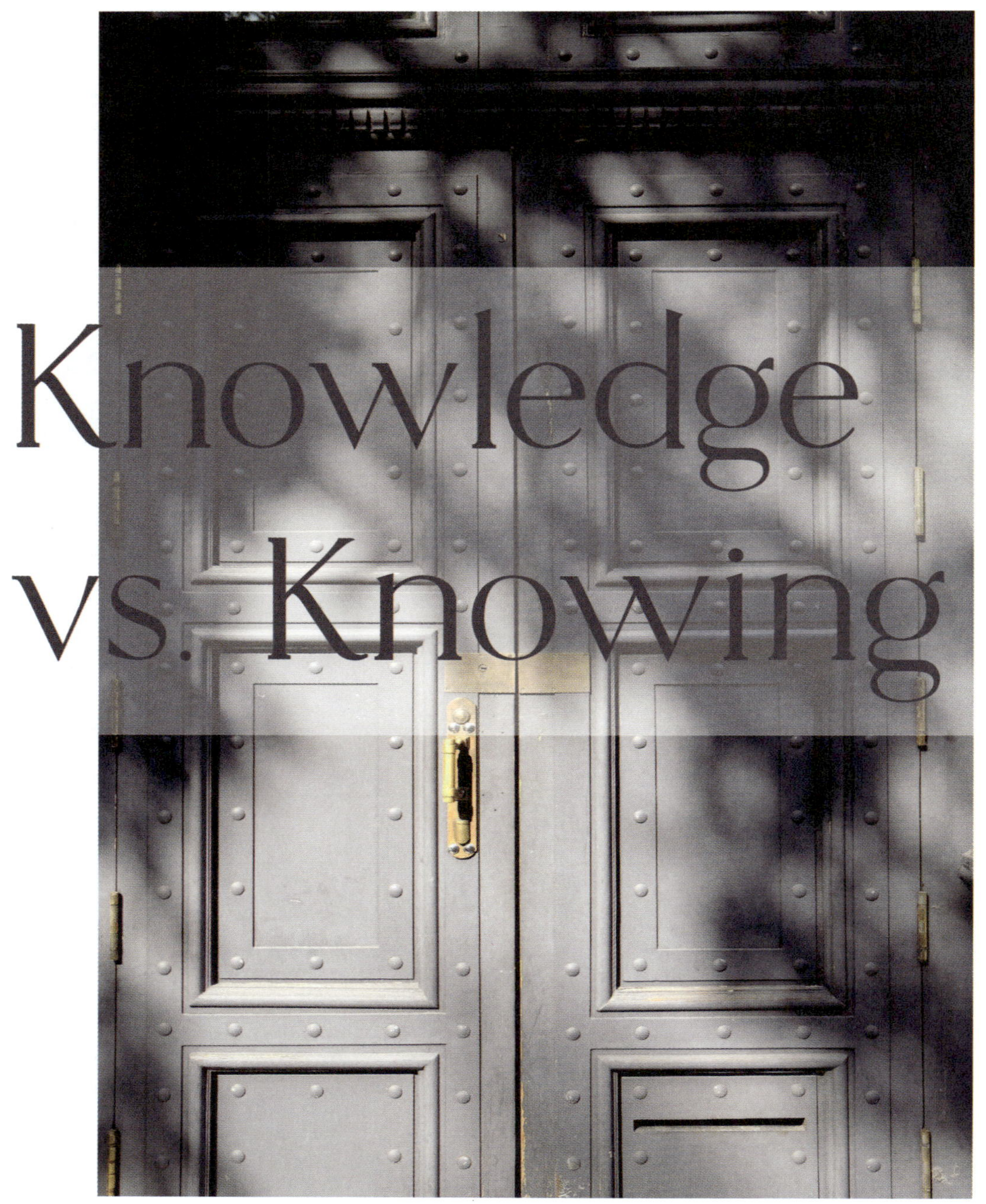
Knowledge
vs. Knowing

Week 1 | Day 3

Knowledge vs. Knowing

The Information Age has offered us knowledge about anyone and anything at our fingertips. I will most likely never meet Great Britain's Prince William and Princess Kate, but I feel like I know them. Over the decades, I've watched William grow up, mourned with him during the funeral of Princess Diana, and celebrated his wedding to Kate. I even follow the adorable royal family on social media. Despite all my attempts, I have knowledge about them, but I don't know them personally.

Our relationship with the triune God can be similar. We hear sermons about the Father, Son, and Holy Spirit. We might even take notes and underline verses in our Bible. We can share at a small group, pray with a friend, and go to church every week but still not know Him.

As Moses and the Children of Israel left Egypt and entered the Promised Land, they visibly saw God's power on display in the most miraculous fashion. The ten plagues, water from the rock, daily manna, and the parting of the Red Sea were witnessed by all Israelites.

But Moses experienced the presence of God in a special way as he sought the face of God, wanting communion with Him. And because of the attitude of Moses's heart, God spoke to him as one would a friend.

Moses's desire to know God was so great that he requested God to show him His "glorious presence" (Exodus 33:18). God graciously answered that request, which was later noted by the psalmist David.

At the very heart of God is His desire to have an intimate, growing relationship with you. No matter your maturity level in Christ, ups and downs are normal in all relationships. And it's the same with Jesus. Press on in your pursuit to know about Him and press in to knowing Him more.

Do you desire to know more of God as Moses did? Why or why not?

____

____

____

____

What are some ways that you can remind yourself of God's presence and to talk with God more frequently throughout your day? How do you feel about conversational prayer with God?

____

____

____

____

Prayer

LORD, REMIND ME OF YOUR PRESENCE THROUGHOUT MY BUSY
DAY. LET ME BE AWARE OF YOUR NEARNESS.

AMEN.

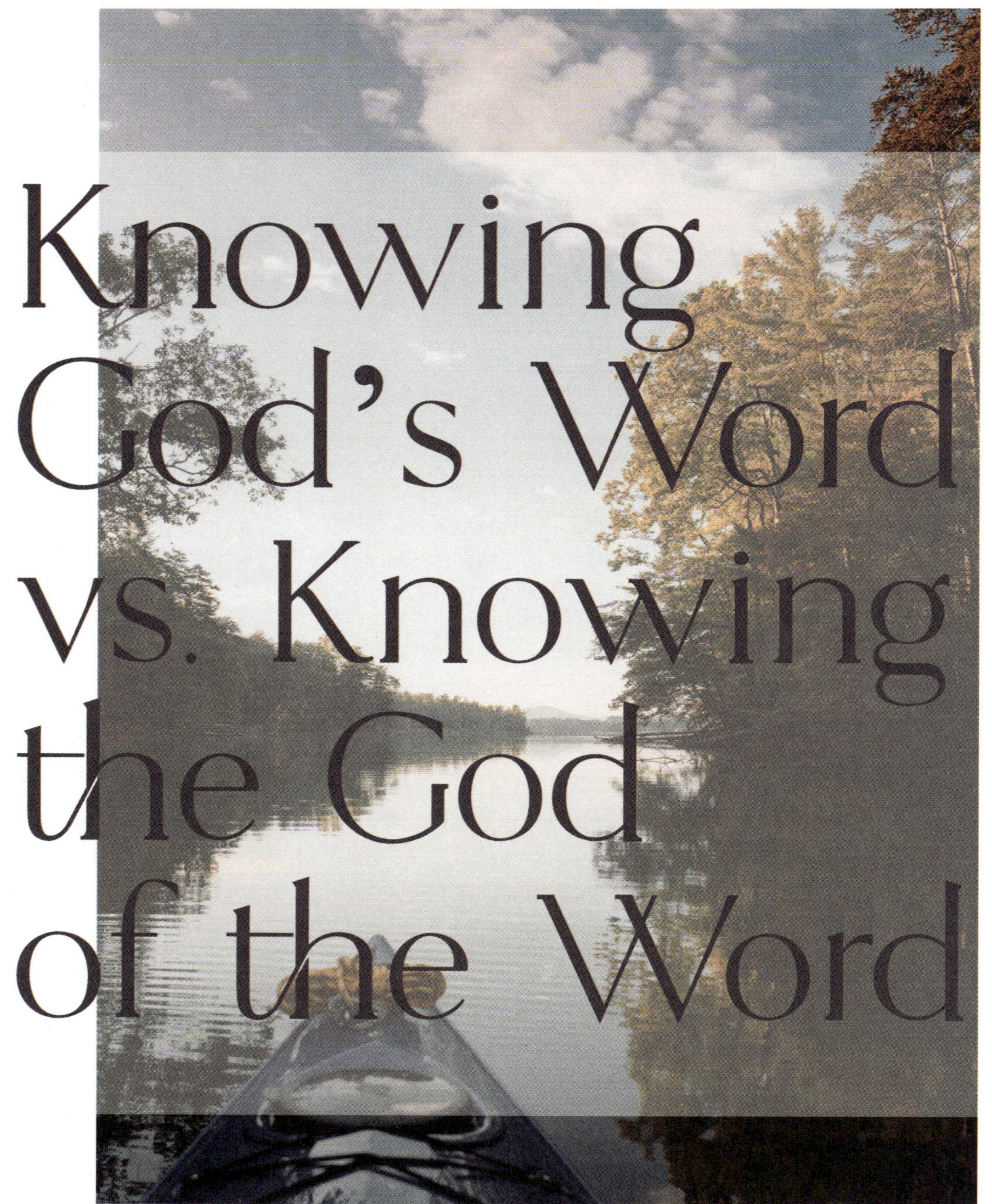

Knowing God's Word vs. Knowing the God of the Word

Week 1 | Day 4

Knowing God's Word vs. Knowing the God of the Word

As a teenager, I loved going to summer camp with my youth group. I grew exponentially each time I dedicated the week to knowing Jesus more. Of course, it was always a lot of fun too. We had team competitions throughout the week, and one way I was able to help my teammates was by memorizing Bible verses. Thanks to those summers, and the incentive of a gazillion points for my team, I'm so thankful that I still remember the Scriptures hidden in my heart from so many years ago.

As Christians, one of the pillars of our theology rests on the belief in the infallibility of the Word of God. Written by men who were inspired by the Holy Spirit, the Bible tells us God's redemption plan for humankind. It is truth from cover to cover.

Jesus is also the Author of our faith (Hebrew 12:2, KJV). While reading the Bible for information is valuable, getting to know the Author is even greater. John wrote, "In the beginning the Word already existed. The Word was with God, and the Word was God. He existed in the beginning with God" (John 1:1). Jesus is the Living Word, and everything about Him points us to the Father so we can walk with Him in close communion, even as Jesus does. With each story penned, the Scripture is revealing the love of God for us. Look at Paul's declaration.

Our faith is not based on merely a culmination of ancient stories; it hinges on the death-defying fact that Jesus rose from the grave. The story is recorded so we may walk this journey of life hand in hand with the Almighty God.

Reflection

This week in your Bible reading, look for ways God is present in the story. Write down the description and begin to keep a list of the characteristics, attributes, and names of God.

Prayer

FATHER, REVEAL YOURSELF TO ME TODAY IN A NEW AND POWERFUL WAY.

AMEN.

A Journey to Knowing God More

Week 1 | Day 5

A Journey To Knowing God More

Standing in front of a roller coaster at an amusement park, I could describe in great detail what I see. I could tell you about the wind I feel on my face when it rushes by. I could tell you about the screams of excitement I hear, the steep, slow climbs, and the exhilarating drops. It looks like fun, but until I get in and buckle up, I am only an observer without firsthand experience.

It's easy to be an observer on your own spiritual journey. Watching the lives of others can leave you jealous that you're missing out or fearful of what God might want you to do.

This week, we have discussed what's required to take steps closer to God and get to know Him more. One thing we haven't discussed is the reality that relationships go both ways. They work best when there is mutual honesty, transparency, authenticity, and trust. As much as we say, "God, I want to know You more," we should include, "God, I want You to know me, too."

David began Psalm 139 by acknowledging that God knew everything about him.

> O LORD, YOU HAVE EXAMINED MY HEART AND KNOW EVERYTHING ABOUT ME. YOU KNOW WHEN I SIT DOWN OR STAND UP. YOU KNOW MY THOUGHTS EVEN WHEN I'M FAR AWAY.
>
> PSALM 139:1–2

Then David went a step further and asked the Lord to reveal what might be hiding unaware in his heart.

> SEARCH ME, O GOD, AND KNOW MY HEART; TEST ME AND KNOW MY ANXIOUS THOUGHTS. POINT OUT ANYTHING IN ME THAT OFFENDS YOU, AND LEAD ME ALONG THE PATH OF EVERLASTING LIFE.
>
> PSALM 139:23–24

It is safe to go to your Heavenly Father with all the issues of your heart. If you have apprehensions about intimacy with Him based on human relationships, let Him heal and redefine your experiences by renewing your ability to trust and love, and to feel safe and valued.

Reflection

Take inventory by searching your heart. Then ask the Lord to search your heart. Write down what is revealed.

____

____

____

____

Confess any sin that the Holy Spirit brings to light. With open hands toward heaven, receive His forgiveness, love, and acceptance. Write down today's date and declare that you are entering a new season of intimacy with the Lord.

____

____

____

____

Prayer

HERE I AM, LORD. I SURRENDER ALL OF ME.
THANK YOU FOR FILLING ME WITH YOUR HOLY SPIRIT
AND WALKING WITH ME EVERY DAY OF MY LIFE.
MAY THE AUTHENTICITY OF MY RELATIONSHIP WITH YOU
SPEAK TO THOSE IN MY LIFE AND DRAW THEM CLOSER TO YOU.

AMEN.

WEEK ONE

As we delve into this journey of knowing God more intimately, what might be some positive benefits to a closer relationship with Him?

____

____

____

____

When you think of a deeper relationship with God, does it bring up any negative feelings, fears, or emotions? If so, what or where is the origin of these feelings?

____

____

____

____

Discuss how human relationships can inadvertently influence our relationship with God. In what ways would an intimate relationship with the Lord differ from human relationships?

____

____

____

____

How would knowing God in a personal way impact us in greater ways as we read, study, and meditate on the Scripture?

____

____

____

____

Share and look up Bible promises that talk about God's desire to know you and His tenacity in pursuing you.

____

____

____

____

WEEK
Two

O LORD, you have
examined my heart and know
everything about me.
You know when I sit down or
stand up. You know my thoughts
even when I'm far away.
You see me when I travel and
when I rest at home.
You know everything I do.
You know what I am going to say
even before I say it, LORD.
You go before me and follow me.
You place your hand of blessing
on my head.

Psalm 139:1–5

Knowing God in My Emotional Life

Week 2 | Day 1

Knowing God in My Emotional Life

Emotions are a gift from God that span from ecstatic joy to the depths of despair. They make us feel alive and give depth to our experiences on earth. We can't fool emotions; they have been known to bubble up and inform our heart and mind of what is going on right under the surface even when we are unaware.

However, not all emotions are the same. Experiencing peace, joy, and happiness make life more enjoyable, while sadness, fear, and anger are emotions not as pleasurable to walk through.

It's important to know where emotions belong in our life and are mindful of the attention we give them. Circumstances can provoke our emotions and then feelings can run wild, which makes them precarious leaders. Being led by emotions is exhausting and can delay or even derail one's purpose and future.

Recorded in the Bible are the trials and troubles of many well-known characters, accompanied by their consequent emotions. David had sorrows. Moses had low self-esteem. Miriam was envious. Peter was fearful.

This week we will look at how God meets us in our emotions. Ultimately, God uses every portion of our life to connect and draw us closer to us. Invite Him into your emotions—positive and negative—and ask Him to reveal a new characteristic of His nature that you've never known before. Let it be an opportunity for growth and deeper understanding of both yourself and the Lord.

Reflection

Make a list of the positive and negative emotions you are experiencing this week. Which emotions are now running (or have in the past run) wild? What was the outcome?

____

____

____

____

Why is willpower alone not enough to control emotions?

____

____

____

____

Prayer

*LORD, I LAY MY EMOTIONS DOWN AT YOUR FEET.
RESTORE, REPAIR, AND REDEEM THE WOUNDED PLACES IN MY
SOUL SO THAT I MAY WALK IN YOUR PEACE AND JOY.
THANK YOU FOR REVEALING YOURSELF TO ME THIS WEEK
IN WAYS I HAVE NEVER KNOWN BEFORE.*

AMEN.

When I
Am Feeling
Afraid

Week 2 | Day 2

When I Am Feeling Afraid

IN ALL YOUR WAYS ACKNOWLEDGE HIM, AND HE SHALL DIRECT YOUR PATHS.

PROVERBS 3:6 (NKJV)

IN ALL YOUR WAYS—WHEN YOUR WAY INCLUDES FEAR
KNOW—EXPERIENTIALLY, INTIMATELY KNOW THIS CHARACTERISTIC OF
HIM—*JEHOVAH-SHAMMAH,* THE LORD IS THERE, THE EVER-PRESENT GOD

Fear is one of the most universal human emotions. There is a healthy fear that makes us cautious and conscientious about our well-being, like when we are afraid to get close to a high ledge or a flame on the stove.

There is another kind of fear that is neither healthy nor helpful, and it originates with the enemy himself. This fear aims to strike terror into the heart and paralyze its victim. But the Lord answers this with His very presence in our life. Isaiah 41:10 instructs us,

"DON'T BE AFRAID, FOR I AM WITH YOU. DON'T BE DISCOURAGED, FOR I AM YOUR GOD. I WILL STRENGTHEN YOU AND HELP YOU. I WILL HOLD YOU UP WITH MY VICTORIOUS RIGHT HAND."

Hundreds of years before Jesus' birth, Isaiah prophesied that He would be called *Immanuel*, which means "God with us" (Isaiah 7:14). Repeatedly, the Lord convinces us of His closeness. In His presence, fear has no power, no authority, and no voice. His nearness relieves our fears and gives us courage to face the day.

Psalm 23:4 reminds us again:

Life happens and brings with it uncertainty and unforeseen changes, which can result in fear. Remember, that through it all, the Lord is with *you*.

He is your ever-present God. Do you know Him?

ADDITIONAL SCRIPTURES ABOUT FEAR
PSALMS 34:4; 139:7; 2 TIMOTHY 1:7; 1 JOHN 4:18

Are you experiencing fear in any area of your life? If so, where?

____

____

____

____

Ask God to reveal any root cause and ask Him to remove it.

____

____

____

____

Week 2 - Day 2

Prayer

LORD, WHEN I HEAR FEAR'S VOICE, HELP ME TO SILENCE IT BY FILLING MY MIND WITH SCRIPTURE. THANK YOU FOR BEING WITH ME WHEN I AM AFRAID AND DELIVERING ME FROM ALL MY FEARS. WITH YOU, I AM STRONG AND COURAGEOUS.

AMEN.

When I Am Feeling Confused

Week 2 | Day 3

When I Am Feeling Confused

Despite our level of maturity, intellect, or experience, there are times when confusion is all we feel. Too many options, not enough options, and the pressure to make the right choice can leave us perplexed and paralyzed to be able to make a decision. To which voice should I listen?

There is a reason why Jesus referred to us as sheep so often in the Gospels. Apparently, sheep are not that bright when it comes to figuring out life for themselves. I can relate! However, where there are sheep, there is a shepherd.

> "I AM THE GOOD SHEPHERD; I KNOW MY OWN
> SHEEP, AND THEY KNOW ME."
>
> JOHN 10:14

When we are confused, one of the smartest responses we can immediately put into action is to follow the Good Shepherd. He knows the way and He will show the way!

Sometimes He will bring wisdom and clarity to dispel the confusion. In those moments, the fog seems to lift and you know exactly what to do. Other times, you may not get a clear answer and will need to trust Him with all the unknowns. In these moments, His peace and comfort can quiet your heart, even when your head is spinning.

Hear His voice and follow His lead by reading the Word and praying. He has made provision along the way that will sustain you through every uncertainty.

> THE Lord IS MY SHEPHERD;
> I HAVE ALL THAT I NEED.
>
> PSALM 23:1

ADDITIONAL SCRIPTURES ABOUT CONFUSION
PSALM 119:169; JEREMIAH 33:3; MATTHEW 7:7-8

Reflection

Write down any area of your life where you are experiencing confusion. Bring it to the Lord and thank Him for bringing clarity to your situation.

____

____

____

____

Ask the Lord to show you any place where you are leading yourself instead of following where He is leading.

____

____

____

____

Prayer

LORD, THANK YOU FOR BEING MY GOOD SHEPHERD. I SURRENDER TO YOUR LEADERSHIP AND CHOOSE TO TRUST AS YOU GUIDE AND PROVIDE FOR ME TODAY. DISPEL MY CONFUSION AND REPLACE IT WITH WISDOM AND PEACE.

AMEN.

When I Am Feeling Disappointed

Week 2 | Day 4

When I Am Feeling Disappointed

IN ALL YOUR WAYS ACKNOWLEDGE HIM, AND HE SHALL DIRECT YOUR PATHS.

PROVERBS 3:6 (NKJV)

IN ALL YOUR WAYS—WHEN YOUR WAY INCLUDES DISAPPOINTMENT
KNOW—EXPERIENTIALLY, INTIMATELY KNOW THIS CHARACTERISTIC OF
HIM—MY HOPE

There comes a time in every believer's life when she wrestles with this thought: *If I might be disappointed in the end, why should I even try to have hope?*

In our natural mind it makes sense. If something doesn't go as you planned, then you're prepared for it. If it does go in the way you planned, then you're pleasantly surprised. However, in an attempt to safeguard your heart, you may bypass God, who gives you a living hope (1 Peter 1:3, NKJV).

King David experienced numerous difficulties and frequently wrote about his disappointments. I think we appreciate him because of his brutal honesty as he talked with God. But after confessing his woes, he always answered his own dilemma by trusting the Lord with fresh hope.

WHY AM I DISCOURAGED? WHY IS MY HEART SO SAD?
I WILL PUT MY HOPE IN GOD!
I WILL PRAISE HIM AGAIN—MY SAVIOR AND MY GOD!

PSALM 42:11

The Lord does not just have hope, He *is* our hope.

> O LORD, YOU ALONE ARE MY HOPE.
>
> PSALM 71:5

Hope is more than wishful thinking, positivity, or optimism. Hope waits with red-hot expectation, because its foundation is rooted in the promises of God. Hope leans in instead of backing out.

And here is something else—hope is fuel for our faith.

> FAITH SHOWS THE REALITY OF WHAT WE HOPE FOR; IT IS THE EVIDENCE OF THINGS WE CANNOT SEE.
>
> HEBREWS 11:1

Take away our hope and we have no faith, which is the means of our salvation and affects every portion of our walk with Jesus. (This points to the reason why the enemy attempts to make us hopeless!)

Even when it doesn't go as we have hoped, hope does not disappoint because Jesus himself is our hope. We don't hope for something, we hope in Someone. We can be at peace knowing that He has something better or different, or the timing is not right.

> Rubem Alves said, "Hope is hearing the music of the future. Faith is the courage to dance to it today."[2]

He is the Lord, your Hope. Do you know Him?

ADDITIONAL SCRIPTURES ABOUT HOPE
PSALM 62:5-6; JEREMIAH 29:11; ROMANS 12:12; 15:13

---

[2]William C. Frey, *The Dance of Hope: Finding Ourselves in the Rhythm of God's Great Story* (Colorado Springs: WaterBrook Press, 2010), 10.

Reflection

Remember a time where you experienced disappointment. Were you able to move on or did it create hopelessness in an area of your life? Take it to the Lord and ask Him to reveal what step you might need to take (i.e., forgiveness, confession, etc).

____

____

____

____

How will knowing the God of hope help you in the future?

____

____

____

____

Prayer

LORD, I GIVE YOU ALL MY DISAPPOINTMENTS, THE TIMES WHEN CIRCUMSTANCES DIDN'T GO MY WAY OR WHEN SOMEONE LET ME DOWN. WHETHER THEY WERE AT FAULT OR NOT, I SURRENDER IT ALL TO YOU. HEAL MY HEART FROM THIS WOUND.

AMEN.

When I Am Feeling Worried

Week 2 | Day 5

When I Am Feeling Worried

IN ALL YOUR WAYS ACKNOWLEDGE HIM, AND HE SHALL DIRECT YOUR PATHS.

PROVERBS 3:6 (NKJV)

IN ALL YOUR WAYS—WHEN YOUR WAY INCLUDES WORRY
KNOW—EXPERIENTIALLY, INTIMATELY KNOW THIS CHARACTERISTIC OF
HIM—FAITHFUL AND TRUE

Worry is an epidemic in our world, even among Christians. Some proudly wear it as a badge of honor and consider it a way of caring. If you love someone, you worry about them, right?

We worry about finances, children, spouses, parents, and jobs. We worry about the past, the present, and the future. We are so good at worrying! It comes naturally and gives the illusion that answers will come from this practice. Holocaust survivor Corrie ten Boom said, "Worry does not empty tomorrow of its sorrow, it empties today of its strength."[3]

---

[3]Corrie ten Boom, *Clippings from My Notebook* (Nashville, TN: Thomas Nelson, 1982), 33.

Jesus himself spoke directly to this topic.

> CAN ALL YOUR WORRIES ADD A SINGLE MOMENT TO YOUR LIFE?
>
> MATTHEW 6:27

Philippians 4:6 continues with this:

> DON'T WORRY ABOUT ANYTHING; INSTEAD PRAY ABOUT EVERYTHING.

Here is the dilemma—How does prayer keep one from worry?

It's not only about the words we are saying in prayer, but more about to whom we are saying them. Revelation 19:11 tells us another name of Jesus, "Faithful and True." He not only does what is faithful and true, but it's who He is.

With this understanding, we can unburden our heart by giving it over to the One who has the means, the power, and the wisdom to handle our concerns. Our portion is to trust and thank Him for what He is doing instead of fretting.

The God of the universe never sleeps nor slumbers. His eye is always on you. Know that He is well able to care for all that concerns you. He who is faithful and true is tending to the issues of your heart. Leave it in His capable hands and don't worry.

He is faithful and true. Do you know Him?

ADDITIONAL SCRIPTURES ABOUT WORRY
PSALM 34:17; MATTHEW 6:25-26; 1 PETER 5:7

Reflection

Identify all the things you are worried about right now.

____

____

____

____

Throughout your day, what will you substitute for worry when it enters your mind?

____

____

____

____

Prayer

*LORD, MAKE ME AWARE WHEN MY MIND DRIFTS TO WORRY. HELP
ME TO IDENTIFY IT, GIVE IT TO YOU, AND REPLACE IT
WITH THANKSGIVING FOR HOW POWERFULLY YOU ARE
WORKING IN MY LIFE.*

AMEN.

Discuss this thought: Emotions are good *followers* but are not good *leaders*. Is this true for you? Why or why not?

____

____

____

____

When negative emotions are running wild, what are some practical ways to bridle or change them?

____

____

____

____

Emotions can be motivating. Talk about how your emotions might fuel your decisions and directives. (e.g., anger over injustice can be fuel to involvement in ministries, groups, or churches to bring a solution).

____

____

____

How can the fruit of the Spirit in Galatians 5:22–23 be implemented when your circumstances and feelings are out of control?

____

____

____

This week we discussed these names of God: my ever-present God, my Shepherd, my Hope, Faithful and True. Share which name currently resonates with you the most and why.

____

____

____

WEEK
Three

Now all glory to God, who
is able, through his mighty
power at work within us,
to accomplish infinitely
more than we might
ask or think.

Ephesians 3:20

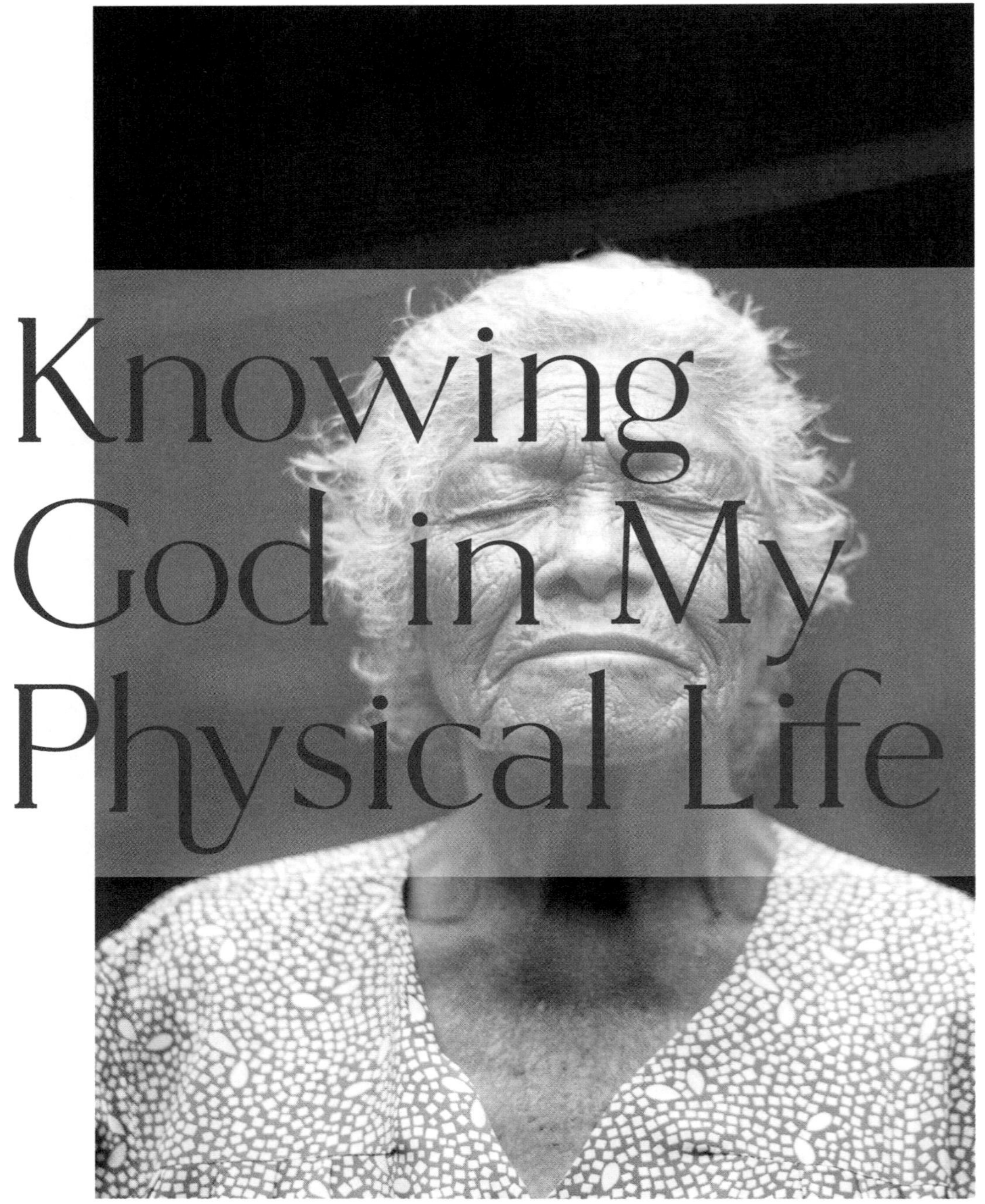

Knowing God in My Physical Life

Week 3 | Day 1

Knowing God in My Physical Life

How amazing to know that we are God's handcrafted, original masterpiece. We are made in the image of our Father, with His very breath giving us life. He has placed us in creation and given us the ability to see the starry sky, hear the birds singing, feel the warmth of sunshine on our face, smell the fragrance of a rose, and taste the sweetness of an orange.

God does not wait for us to get to heaven to meet us where we live. He sent Jesus to earth in human form to identify with us and reconcile us to Him. God cares about our physical frailties, understands our limitations, and invades our reality with His supernatural power and presence.

Sometimes our shortcomings provide opportunities for the Lord to reveal himself to us in new and tangible ways. When you have knocked on every door, talked with everyone you know, and racked your brain to find an answer, He has solutions that you could never imagine.

Where heaven touches earth, it can be a place of miracles, signs, and wonders. God may use people, modern medicine, or do something completely supernatural. Whatever the means, it is the spiritual realm affecting the natural realm. He is a completely supernatural and yet practical God.

This week, we will look at how God meets us in our physical life. Remove familiar limitations and remember that God can show up anywhere, at any time, and in any way. Lean in with eager expectation, knowing that He will bring an answer. Who knows, it might be today!

NOW ALL GLORY TO GOD, WHO IS ABLE, THROUGH HIS MIGHTY POWER AT WORK WITHIN US, TO ACCOMPLISH INFINITELY MORE THAN WE MIGHT ASK OR THINK.

EPHESIANS 3:20

Reflection

What struggles in your physical life are you experiencing right now?
List how your current problems can be seen as an opportunity to
grow and mature.

____

____

____

____

Make two lists—what you can do and what only God can do.

____

____

____

____

Prayer

*LORD, I LAY MY PHYSICAL LIFE AT YOUR FEET. YOU KNOW MY
EVERYDAY NEEDS AND I ASK YOU TO MEET THEM THIS WEEK.
HELP ME TO TRUST YOU IN NEW WAYS AND GIVE ME THE PEACE
THAT PASSES UNDERSTANDING AS I WAIT ON YOU. THANK YOU FOR
REVEALING YOURSELF TO ME THIS WEEK IN WAYS I HAVE NEVER
KNOWN BEFORE.*

AMEN.

When I Am Experiencing Lack

Week 3 | Day 2

When I Am Experiencing Lack

Some days don't seem to have enough of what we need or want. Our immediate thoughts may go to finances, but we also experience lack in other areas. Often, we feel as though we don't have enough time, energy, rest, or even help. There are times when even our self-esteem suffers, and we don't feel like we ourself are enough.

The answer begins with knowing God is the source of everything and we bring little to the equation. He made it all and owns it all. He is the Giver of it all, from life to breath to the heavens and the earth. It all belongs to Him.

And since everything is His to distribute, it is fitting that His name is the Lord who provides. In the Hebrew language, *jireh* has an even deeper meaning. It conveys "the Lord will see to it." When the person who has the authority and power to make something happen is "seeing to it," doesn't that bring peace to your heart?

Genesis 22 tells the story of God testing Abraham by telling him to sacrifice his son Isaac. Without hesitation, Abraham obeyed the Lord; he packed up, chopped wood, and journeyed to the place of sacrifice.

Seeing the wood and the fire, Isaac questioned his father concerning the missing sacrifice. Abraham's response was, "God will provide a sheep for the burnt offering, my son" (verse 8).

Abraham did not know how God would bring a solution, but he knew that He would. At the moment of sacrifice, the Lord called out to Abraham to go no further. He had passed the test. The Lord provided a ram in the thicket for the sacrifice. Abraham called that place "the LORD will provide" (verse 14).

The place of lack is the place to get acquainted with God, your Provider. You might not know how or when, but the Lord will see to it.

He is the Lord, your Provider. Do you know Him?

Reflection

Do you believe your Good Father is a Good Provider? Why or why not?

____

____

____

____

When you are experiencing lack in an area of your life, what are some practical ways that you can trust God until you see your breakthrough?

____

____

____

____

Prayer

LORD, YOUR WORD SAYS THAT IF YOU LOOK AFTER THE SPARROWS AND DRESS THE LILLIES, SURELY YOU WILL TAKE CARE OF ME (MATTHEW 6:25-30). I GIVE YOU MY NEED AND THANK YOU FOR YOUR ANSWERS THAT ARE ON THE WAY. YOU ARE ABLE AND I KNOW YOU WILL SEE TO IT.

AMEN.

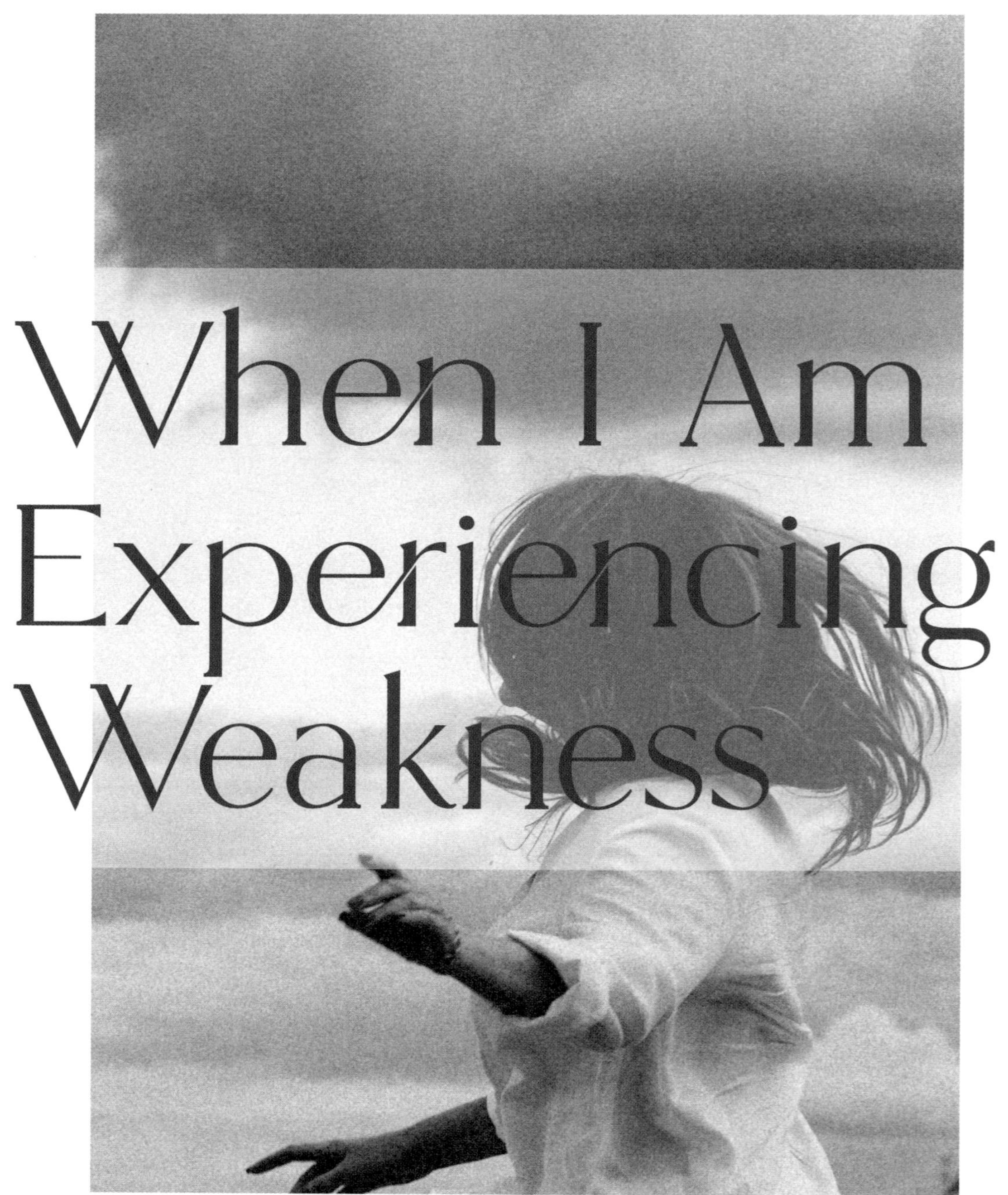
When I Am
Experiencing
Weakness

Week 3 | Day 3

When I Am Experiencing Weakness

Even a child loves to advise his or her parents, "I can do it by myself!" As adults, there is nothing wrong with using our physical and mental strength to progress in every area of life. However, when those areas are weakened for whatever reason, it limits what we can accomplish. Our mind wants to push forward, but at times, we are unable to make it happen.

Abram was seventy-five years old when God told him to leave his home country and promised to make of him a great nation (Genesis 12). At that time, he was childless, but he believed God and obeyed His command.

Genesis 17:1 records Abram's progress twenty-four years later.

Abram was older, much older, undoubtedly weaker, and still childless. Sarai, his wife, was also much older and past the time of childbearing. At this time, God did two interesting things: He told Abram that His name is *El-Shaddai* and then He changed Abram's name (meaning exalted father) to Abraham (meaning father of many nations). Miraculously, one year later, when Abraham was one hundred years old, Isaac was born.

When you find yourself losing strength and unable to accomplish something because of increasing weakness, this is where you meet your Almighty God. His strength and power are matchless, and they never wane. It is in these trying moments that He wants us to do our part, while He does His part.

We give thanks to God for the ability to do things in our strength, but something supernatural is set in motion when we are operating from a place of weakness. Our weakness, coupled with our obedience, creates a space for Almighty God to be praised. When it is beyond our physical or mental capability, this is when God receives all the glory.

It is easy to equate weakness with defeat and failure. But the Lord sees it as an opportunity for the miraculous and for us to experience His strength and power in our life. He is attracted to our weakness and frequently demonstrates himself there (2 Corinthians 12:9).

He is your Almighty God. Do you know Him?

ADDITIONAL SCRIPTURES ABOUT GOD'S STRENGTH
2 SAMUEL 22:3; PSALM 27:1; MATTHEW 19:26; PHILIPPIANS 4:13

Reflection

How does experiencing physical, emotional, mental, or spiritual weakness make you feel?

____

____

____

____

What does it look like to substitute God's strength for your weakness?

____

____

____

____

Week 3 - Day 3

Prayer

When I Am Experiencing Illness

Week 3 | Day 4

When I Am Experiencing Illness

IN ALL YOUR WAYS ACKNOWLEDGE HIM, AND HE SHALL DIRECT YOUR PATHS.

PROVERBS 3:6 (NKJV)

IN ALL YOUR WAYS—WHEN YOUR WAY INCLUDES ILLNESS
KNOW—EXPERIENTIALLY, INTIMATELY KNOW THIS CHARACTERISTIC OF
HIM—*JEHOVAH RAPHA,* MY HEALER

Should I bother the Lord when I have a headache? Do I wait and ask for healing only when it's something worse? Does He still heal today or was that for the early disciples? What should we believe if we don't receive a healing miracle?

Most everyone has processed through at least a couple of these questions. And it's good to know that God is not afraid of our hard questions. Search the Bible and see the theme of healing from cover to cover.

In Exodus 15:26, we have our answer. "I am the LORD who heals you." More accurately, He is not just the God who heals, but our God, the Healer. Distinguishing the difference is the key to knowing God and growing in your relationship with Him. He does not just have our healing; He is our Healer.

When we seek the Person instead of the outcome, it helps us to reconcile if healing does not happen in the manner we asked. Living fully surrendered to God means that He is Lord of our life, so we submit our will to His. He is full of compassion and love for us, so whatever the outcome, we can trust Him.

But don't just limit Him to healing bodies. He heals broken hearts and minds, so we don't have to relive trauma and suffer every day. He heals our eyes to see with new perspective, to give us a future and a hope (Jeremiah 29:11). He can heal the pains from our past and set us free to walk into a bright future.

Divine healing is a supernatural provision and promise of God. Whether it is internal or external, whatever "open wound" or "broken bone" you are nursing, the Healer wants to mend it.

He is the Lord, your Healer. Do you know Him?

ADDITIONAL SCRIPTURES ON HEALING
PSALMS 103:3; 147:3; JAMES 5:15; 1 PETER 2:24

Is there a place in your body, your mind, your heart, or your soul that needs healing? Describe it here.

____

____

____

____

Make a list of the ways God has healed you in the past. Let it remind you that He did it before, and He can do it again.

____

____

____

____

THANK YOU, LORD, FOR BEING MY HEALER. I BELIEVE THAT BY JESUS' STRIPES, I AM HEALED (ISAIAH 53:5). I TRUST IN YOUR TIMING AND YOUR WAYS FOR IT TO COME.

AMEN.

When I Am Experiencing Loss

Week 3 | Day 5

When I Am Experiencing Loss

IN ALL YOUR WAYS ACKNOWLEDGE HIM, AND HE SHALL DIRECT YOUR PATHS.

PROVERBS 3:6 (NKJV)

IN ALL YOUR WAYS—WHEN YOUR WAY INCLUDES LOSS
KNOW—EXPERIENTIALLY, INTIMATELY KNOW THIS CHARACTERISTIC OF
HIM—*JEHOVAH RAPHA,* MY VINE

There are seasons of addition and even multiplication in life. Harvest season is wonderful and rewarding, but it does not continue all year round. To produce a healthy and abundant crop, the work begins in the offseason with pruning.

Cutting back a beautiful vine seems counterproductive. How can less turn into more? But it is a law of the harvest. Removing some of the branches helps the remaining branches to grow strong and vibrant, producing better and greater amounts of fruit.

In the same way, seasons of subtraction can be painful. It might be material things or a person who has been removed from your life. Maybe it is a character trait or habit that the Lord is telling you to sever. Whatever it may be, it's easy to be confused, blame yourself, and hold onto the very thing that you don't want to lose.

Instead, this is the very time to cling to Jesus. In John 15:5, He taught His disciples,

> "YES, I AM THE VINE; YOU ARE THE BRANCHES. THOSE WHO REMAIN IN ME, AND I IN THEM, WILL PRODUCE MUCH FRUIT. FOR APART FROM ME YOU CAN DO NOTHING."

Be nourished by His Word. Drink in the Living Water. Be encouraged in His presence and anchored by His roots. Scarcity becomes an opportunity to strengthen and grow.

Be careful, for seasons of loss can make a permanent, negative impact on your life. Processing grief without wise counsel and apart from the Lord can create new growth in the area of bitterness. The Bible refers to bitterness as a root that goes down deep to your very foundation. And you know that a bitter root creates bitter fruit.

How wonderful to know that you are not flailing through life alone but are strongly connected to the Vine who supplies everything you need to flourish. In times of loss and leanness, remember that right behind winter is springtime, where new growth, maturity, and exponential growth is seen.

He is the Lord, your Vine. Do you know Him?

ADDITIONAL SCRIPTURES ON VINES
JOHN 15:1-8

When you are connected to the Vine, Jesus, how does it make you feel? When you are *not* connected to the Vine, how does it make you feel?

____

____

____

____

What can you do today that will strengthen your connection to Him?

____

____

____

____

Prayer

LORD, I WANT TO ABIDE IN YOU. WHEN I'M COMING IN, WHEN I'M GOING OUT, WHEN I'M ASLEEP, AND WHEN I'M AWAKE, HELP ME TO REMAIN IN YOUR WORD, IN YOUR PRESENCE, AND IN YOUR LOVE.

AMEN.

WEEK THREE

Whether you are waiting for a financial miracle, a physical healing, or another area of provision from the Lord, how do you stay faithful and faith-filled as you wait?

____

____

____

____

Look at Matthew 6. Jesus told the crowd that God cares for the birds and the flowers, so we should not worry that He will care for us since we are more valuable. What are ways to combat worry?

____

____

____

____

When God's answer is opposite from how you prayed, how do you accept
His response and not become bitter or angry?

____

____

____

____

Remaining connected to Jesus affects every area of your life. What are
ways that you feel close to the Lord—in nature, in exuberant worship, in
solitude, and, in silence? How can you incorporate these practices into
your life to foster a closer relationship with Him?

____

____

____

____

This week, we discussed these names of God: my Provider, Almighty God,
my Healer, the Vine. Share which name currently resonates with you the
most and why.

____

____

____

____

WEEK

Four

"'You must love the Lord your God
with all your heart, all your soul,
and all your mind.'
This is the first and
greatest commandment.
A second is equally important:
'Love your neighbor as yourself.'
The entire law and all the
demands of the prophets are
based on these two
commandments."

Matthew 22:37–40

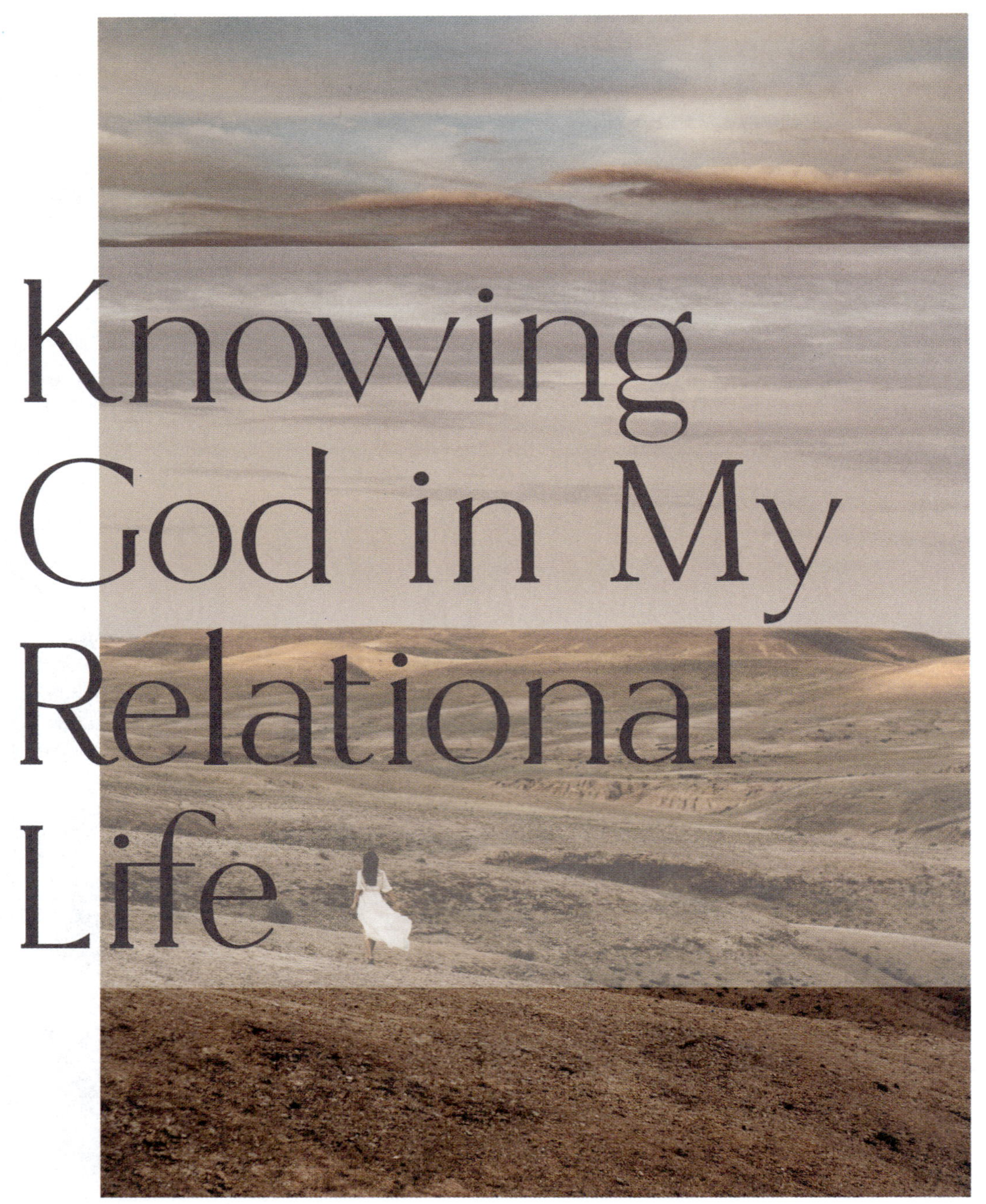

Knowing God in My Relational Life

Week 4 | Day 1

Knowing God in My Relational Life

Everything we experience in this life is meant to be in relationship with God and others. The very reason Jesus went to the Cross was to restore the relationship of sinful people with the Holy God.

Our relationship with Jesus is of primary importance, but following closely behind is our relationship with others. Jesus had much to say about this. Of the 613 Jewish laws, Jesus reduced them down to two:

> "'YOU MUST LOVE THE LORD YOUR GOD WITH ALL YOUR HEART, ALL YOUR SOUL, AND ALL YOUR MIND.' THIS IS THE FIRST AND GREATEST COMMANDMENT. A SECOND IS EQUALLY IMPORTANT: 'LOVE YOUR NEIGHBOR AS YOURSELF.' THE ENTIRE LAW AND ALL THE DEMANDS OF THE PROPHETS ARE BASED ON THESE TWO COMMANDMENTS."
>
> MATTHEW 22:37-40

God cares deeply about our interpersonal connections and wants to reveal characteristics of His nature that pertain specifically to this area. Inviting the Lord into our relationships with our spouse, family, friends, authorities, and even strangers allows us to change our perspective toward others and grow closer to Him.

The first step to deepening your relationship with the Lord comes from you! How can you take a step closer to Him? It may be getting quiet in His presence, meditating on the Word, or spending time in prayer and intercession. All relationships take effort and are built on trust. As your relationship with the Lord grows, it will impact your relationship with others.

This week we will look at common factors in our relationships and explore more names and characteristics of God that will bring comfort and hope.

Reflection

Make a list of your various relationships. What are some of your positive behaviors in each relationship? What are some negative qualities that you exhibit in your relationships?

____

____

____

____

List three things that you can work on in your relationships this week. What are three areas in which you can strengthen your relationship with the Lord?

____

____

____

____

Prayer

LORD, I LAY MY RELATIONSHIPS AT YOUR FEET. I THANK YOU FOR THE PEOPLE IN MY LIFE WHO LOVE AND CARE FOR ME, AS WELL AS THE ONES WHO ARE CHALLENGING. I ASK YOU TO REVEAL YOURSELF TO ME IN WAYS I HAVE NEVER KNOWN BEFORE. SHOW ME WHO YOU ARE IN THE MIDST OF MY RELATIONSHIPS.

AMEN.

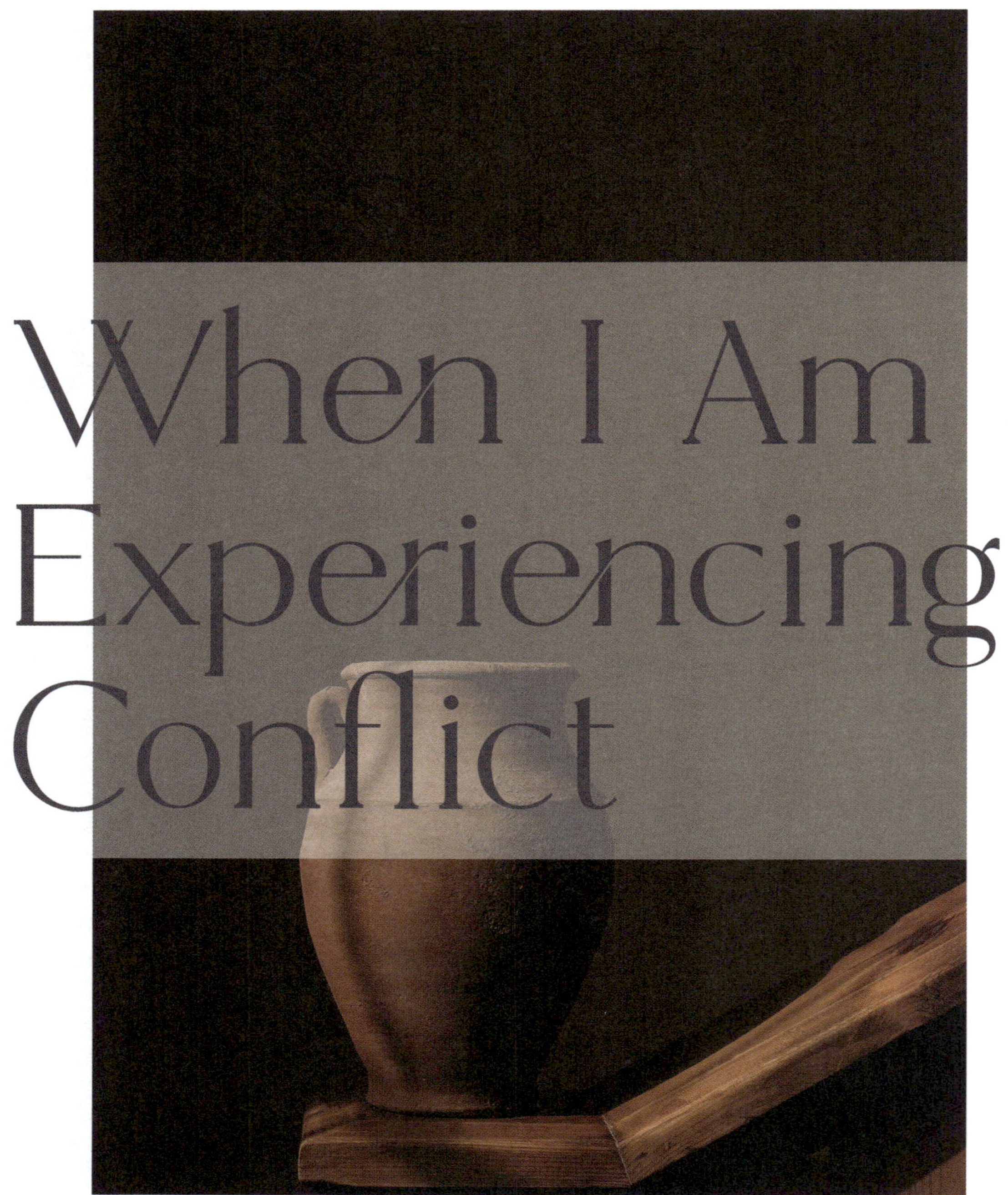

When I Am Experiencing Conflict

Week 4 | *Day 2*

When I Am Experiencing Conflict

IN ALL YOUR WAYS—WHEN YOUR WAY INCLUDES CONFLICT
KNOW—EXPERIENTIALLY, INTIMATELY KNOW THIS CHARACTERISTIC OF
HIM—*JEHOVAH SHALOM,* THE GOD OF PEACE

Disagreement, differences of opinion, and disputes happen in all relationships regardless of their length, strength, or health. At the least, conflict can interrupt harmony in a relationship; at its worst, it results in war.

In Judges 6, the Israelites faced a fierce enemy. The Midianites ravaged entire Israelite villages, taking their livestock, destroying crops, and leaving them to starve. Their reign of terror continued for seven years, until the Lord appeared to an unsuspecting man.

As Gideon hid from the enemy, threshing wheat in a winepress, the angel of the Lord appeared to him. The announcement included an assurance the Lord was with him and a title of "hero" as God sent him on a mission to rescue Israel from the Midianites (Judges 6:11–15).

Gideon pushed back on it all.

He had some valid points! Gideon had conflict with an enemy, conflict in his family, and his own inner conflict.

When Gideon realized that it was God, everything changed. He built an altar and called it *Yahweh-Shalom*, which means "the Lord is peace" (verse 24). The Lord of peace was present amid the conflict and made a difference in the lives of Gideon and the Israelites.

Although conflict resolution is our hope and goal, it doesn't always turn out that way. The key is inviting the God of peace into our relationships, realizing that we cannot change anyone else, only ourself. Relationships can be stormy, but we can remain peaceful as we know more fully the God of peace.

He is the Lord, your peace. Do you know Him?

ADDITIONAL SCRIPTURES ABOUT PEACE
ISAIAH 26:3; PHILIPPIANS 4:6-7; COLOSSIANS 3:15;
2 THESSALONIANS 3:16

What is your typical reaction to conflict? What would be your desired response?

____

____

____

____

How does knowing the Lord, your Peace, change your view of controversy?

____

____

____

____

Prayer

LORD, YOU ARE MY PEACE THROUGH THE STORM. YOU CAN CALM THE SEAS, BUT EVEN IF YOU DON'T, YOU CAN CALM ME. THANK YOU FOR KEEPING ME IN PERFECT PEACE, AS I KEEP MY MIND FOCUSED ON YOU (ISAIAH 26:3).

AMEN.

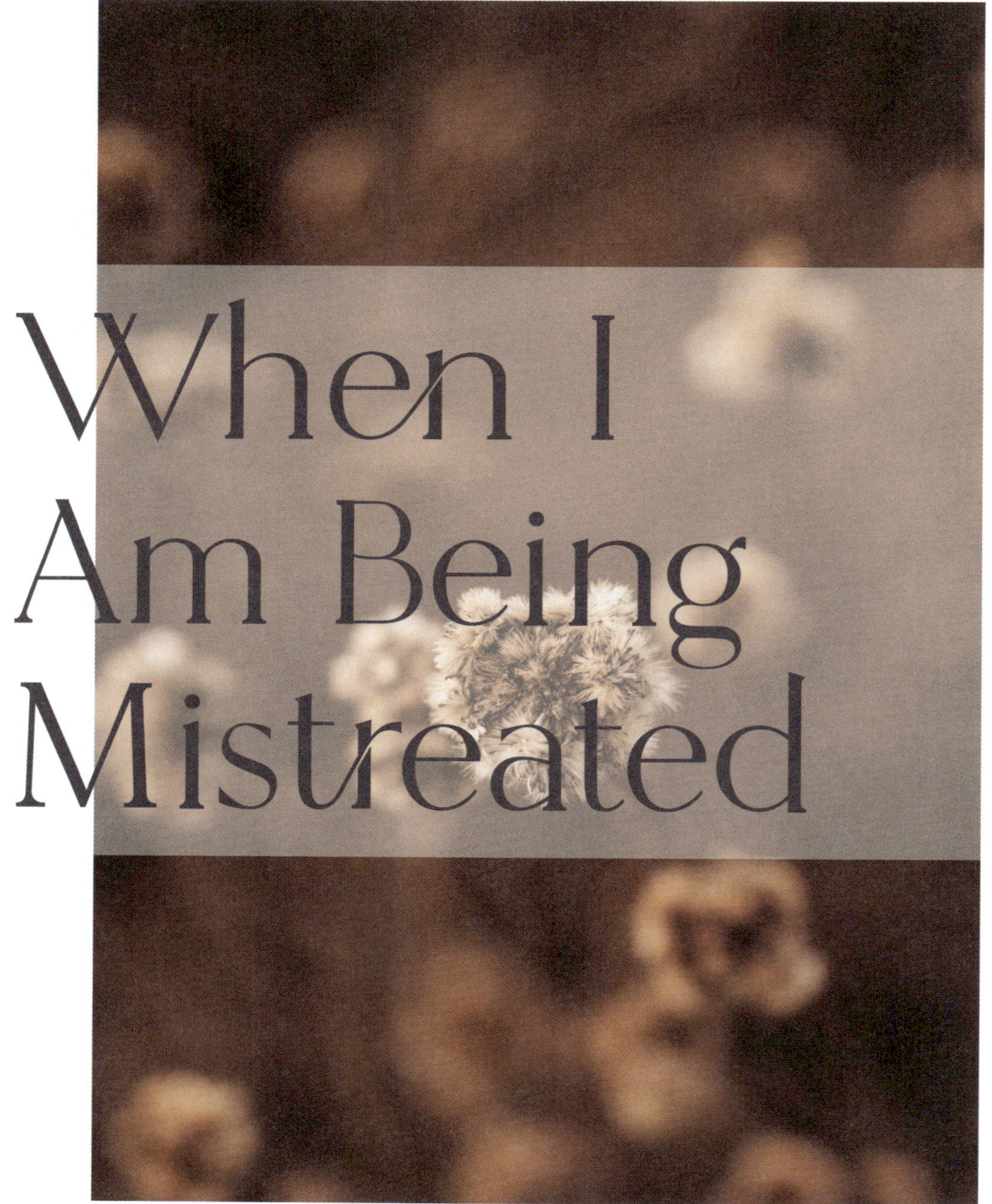

When I
Am Being
Mistreated

Week 4 | Day 3

When I Am Being Mistreated

IN ALL YOUR WAYS ACKNOWLEDGE HIM, AND HE SHALL DIRECT YOUR PATHS.

PROVERBS 3:6 (NKJV)

IN ALL YOUR WAYS—WHEN YOUR WAY INCLUDES MISTREATMENT
KNOW—EXPERIENTIALLY, INTIMATELY KNOW THIS CHARACTERISTIC OF
HIM—*EL-ROI,* THE GOD WHO SEES ME

A boss at work, a teacher at school, a parent, a peer, or a stranger— being mistreated can happen in any relationship. The closer and longer the relationship, the more it hurts. Like a punch to the gut, it can take the wind right out of you when someone you once trusted suddenly responds with unfair treatment, slander, prejudice, or betrayal.

What do we do with all the hurt and injustice?

God told Abraham that he was to be the father of many nations, even though his wife Sarah was barren. Before Isaac, the promised child, was born, there were many years of wondering and waiting in between, and the couple's patience wore thin.

During a particularly doubt-filled moment, Sarah decided to take matters into her own hands by offering her Egyptian servant, Hagar, as a surrogate. Hagar obeyed her mistress, slept with Abraham, and became pregnant. When she realized she was pregnant, Hagar began treating Sarah with contempt. Sarah became incensed with Hagar, treating her "so harshly that she finally ran away" (Genesis 16:6).

As pregnant Hagar was in the barren wilderness, the angel of the Lord visited her. He told her to return to Sarah and name her unborn son Ishmael, which means "God hears." The great expression of compassion from the Lord caused Hagar to call the Lord, *El-roi*, the God who sees me (verse 13).

Like Hagar, when we are being unfairly treated, our first instinct might be to run and escape the situation altogether. We might think of retaliation or feel so oppressed that we cower and recoil. It may feel lonely and like nobody cares, but that is not the truth. Our God, *El-roi*, has His eye on us and is with us. He has counsel, direction, and hope for our future.

Many treated Jesus unfairly, yet He did not retaliate, choosing to trust in God to judge fairly (1 Peter 2:23). He directed us to love our enemies (Matthew 5:44). We are instructed not to return evil for evil, but to overcome evil by doing good (Romans 12:17–21). Knowing the God who sees us, along with the power of the Holy Spirit in us, helps us to treat others as Jesus would treat them and sets a good course for the future.

He is the Lord who sees me. Do you know Him?

NOTE When mistreatment turns into physical abuse, it crosses the line. Your safety, or the safety of others around you, is most important. Seek counsel and ask for help. National Domestic Violence Hotline: 1-800-799-7233

ADDITIONAL SCRIPTURES ABOUT GOD'S WATCHFUL EYE
2 CHRONICLES 16:9; PSALMS 33:18; 121:8

Reflection

When someone is unkind to you, how do you "turn the other cheek" (Matthew 5:39)?

____

____

____

____

How do you trust the Lord while not becoming bitter?

____

____

____

____

Prayer

LORD, YOU SEE IT ALL. YOU KNOW EVERY PART OF THIS UNJUST SITUATION. PROTECT MY HEART FROM LASHING OUT AS I ACTIVELY TRUST THAT YOU ARE WORKING ON MY BEHALF. LIKE HAGAR, MAY THE FRUIT FROM MY LIFE BE A DECLARATION THAT THE LORD HEARS.

AMEN.

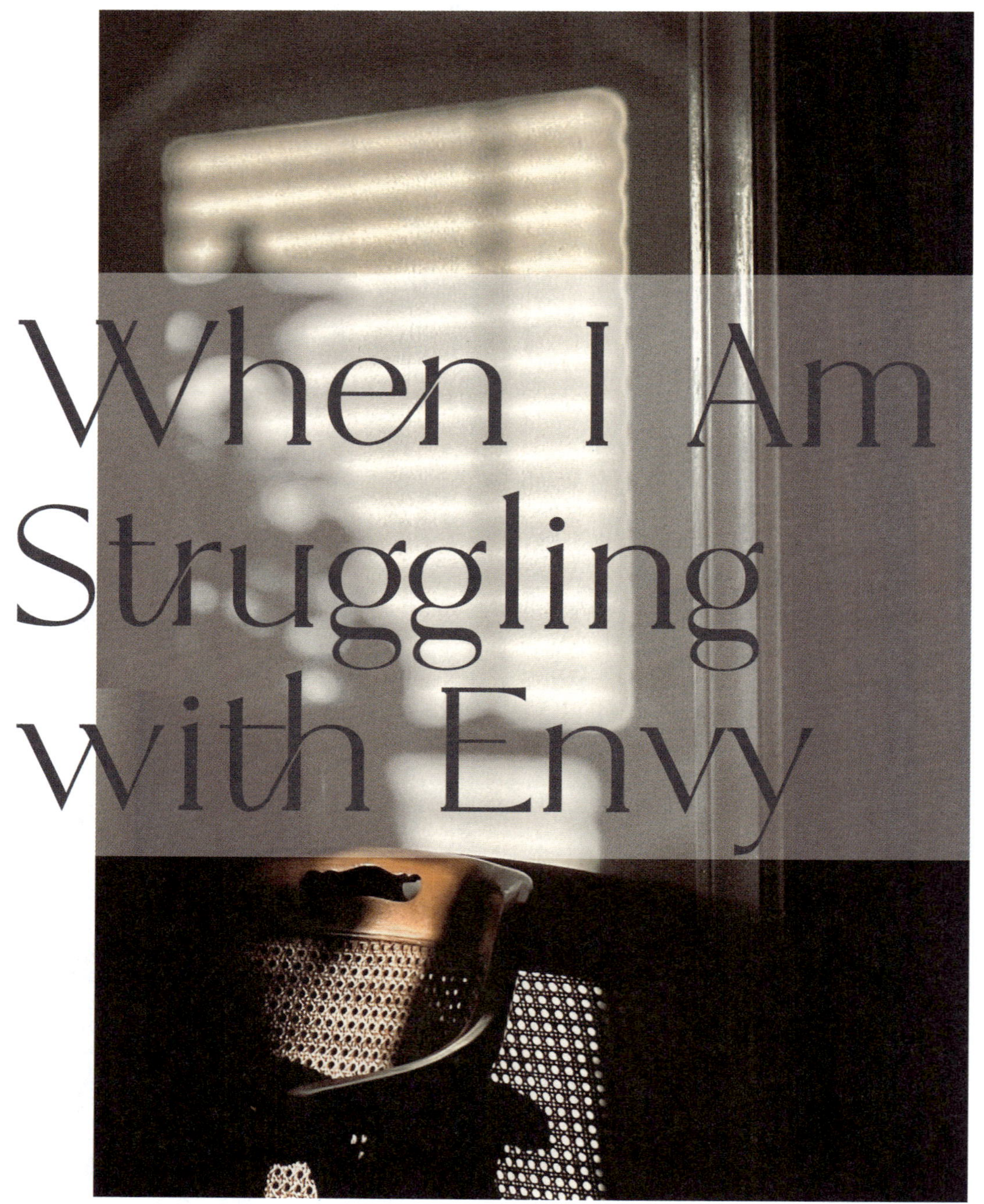
When I Am
Struggling
with Envy

Week 4 | Day 4

When I Am Struggling with Envy

IN ALL YOUR WAYS ACKNOWLEDGE HIM, AND HE SHALL DIRECT YOUR PATHS.

PROVERBS 3:6 (NKJV)

IN ALL YOUR WAYS—WHEN YOUR WAY INCLUDES ENVY
KNOW—EXPERIENTIALLY, INTIMATELY KNOW THIS CHARACTERISTIC OF
HIM—THE LORD, MY STRENGTH

There is a reason why envy made the infamous list of seven deadly sins and the Ten Commandments (coveting is fueled by envy). We don't often talk about it, but identifying it will keep us from grief.

Envy is defined as the feeling of discontent due to desiring a quality or possessions of another. Instead of being content with what we have, we are enticed by someone else's success, possessions, or relationships.

One of the most quoted verses in the Bible is in answer to how we find contentment.

I CAN DO EVERYTHING THROUGH CHRIST, WHO GIVES ME STRENGTH.

PHILIPPIANS 4:13

This supernatural infusion of holy strength is given to us not just to get through life's challenges and victories, but to actually experience contentment and avert the temptation to be envious.

For Paul, it did not matter if life was good or bad, if he had provision or was experiencing lack, if he was in good health or healing from a beating, or was free to travel or locked in prison. Contentment was his default setting, relying on the strength of God to see him through whatever the day would bring (Philippians 4:11–13).

The Greek definition of contentment brings further clarification as to how Paul lived his life and fulfilled his calling. Surprisingly, it describes one who is self-sufficient and independent of external circumstances. Here is the key: Paul was not self-reliant but fully dependent on Christ who dwelt within him by the Holy Spirit. Paul's heart and mind were at peace knowing both the God of strength and the strength of God.

Included in the victory song of Moses is this verse:

> "THE Lord IS MY STRENGTH AND MY SONG; HE HAS GIVEN ME VICTORY."
>
> EXODUS 15:2

Envy is not a motivating factor for future success, but it feeds a constant straining and striving for more. Envy always has an outward focus. Instead, look inward to identify the issue and look upward to call on the Lord, who is your Strength. Contentment is a surrendered heart that experiences peace in the hard things and can thank the God of strength for it all.

He is the Lord, your Strength. Do you know Him?

ADDITIONAL SCRIPTURES ABOUT STRENGTH
PSALM 46:1–3; ISAIAH 40:31; EPHESIANS 6:10

Reflection

Discontent breeds grumbling and complaining. Identify any areas where discontent has snuck into your heart.

____

____

____

____

How do you guard your heart against envy?

____

____

____

____

Prayer

LORD, I'M SORRY FOR MY DISCONTENT AND ENVIOUS HEART.
FORGIVE ME AND CLEANSE ME FROM MY SIN. HELP ME TO HAVE
AN ATTITUDE OF GRATITUDE THROUGHOUT MY DAY
AND EVERY DAY.

AMEN.

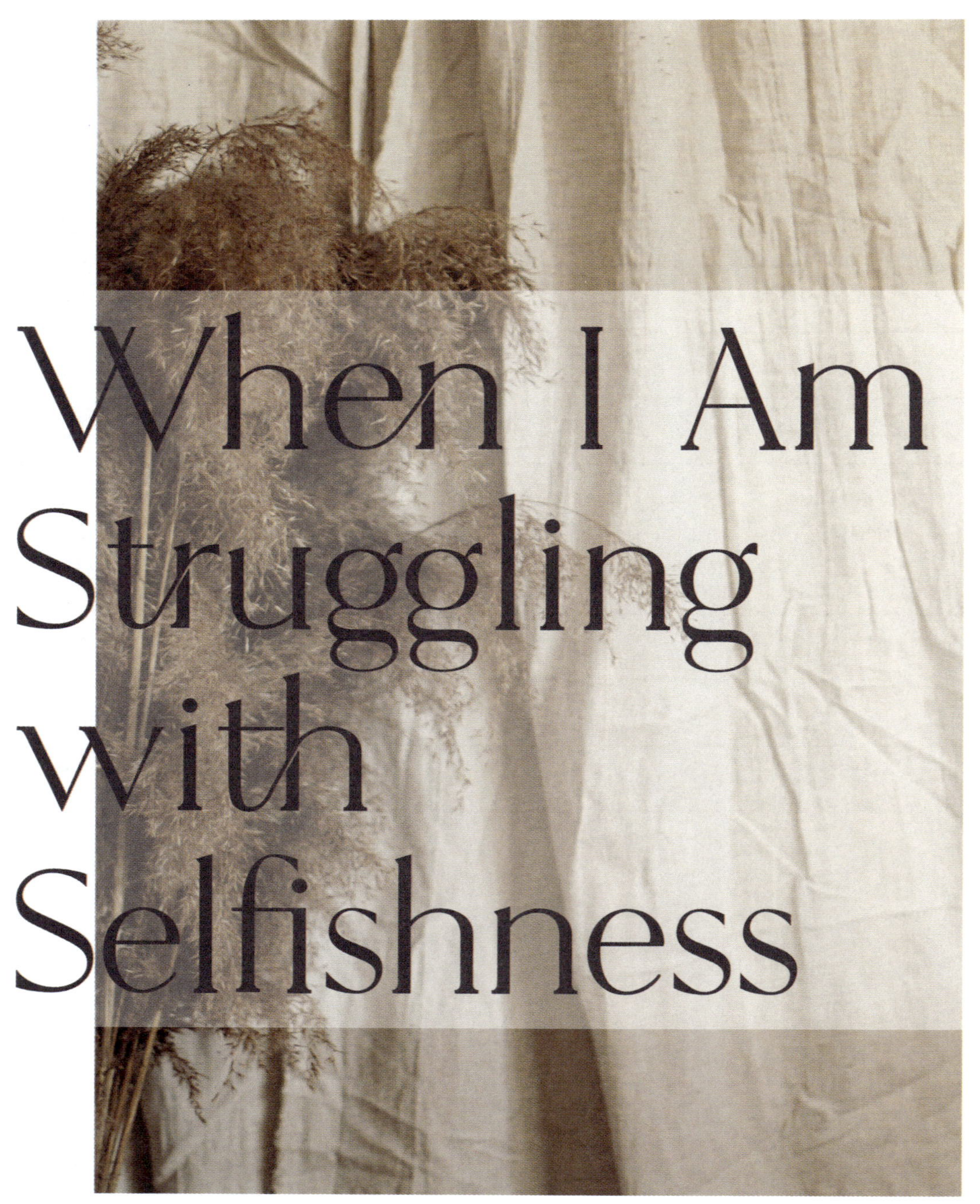

When I Am Struggling with Selfishness

Week 4 | Day 5

When I Am Struggling with Selfishness

IN ALL YOUR WAYS ACKNOWLEDGE HIM, AND HE SHALL DIRECT YOUR PATHS.

PROVERBS 3:6 (NKJV)

IN ALL YOUR WAYS—WHEN YOUR WAY INCLUDES SELFISHNESS
KNOW—EXPERIENTIALLY, INTIMATELY KNOW THIS CHARACTERISTIC OF
HIM—THE SERVANT

"Mine!" is typically one of the first words that babies learn to say. There's no need to work at being selfish; it is innate and comes quite naturally from the minute we enter this realm of flesh and blood. Galatians even lists selfishness among other evil desires our sinful nature craves (Galatians 5:19–21).

Selfishness is a behavior or attitude that is primarily concerned with one's own interests or welfare, often at the expense of others. The business world, politics, and culture abundantly reflect selfishness when it is left unchecked and running wild. Even when people begin a career with altruistic motives, self-serving and self-focused practices can creep into their lives.

If selfishness is being inward focused, the opposite is being outward and others focused. This is expressed through service. Jesus is the supreme model of serving others. Matthew 12:18 records when Jesus fulfilled the messianic prophesy found in Isaiah 42:1:

> "LOOK AT MY SERVANT, WHOM I HAVE CHOSEN.
> HE IS MY BELOVED, WHO PLEASES ME."

Later, Jesus described in greater detail what His being a servant entailed.

> "FOR EVEN THE SON OF MAN CAME NOT TO BE
> SERVED BUT TO SERVE OTHERS AND TO GIVE HIS
> LIFE AS A RANSOM FOR MANY."
> MATTHEW 20:28

In sharp contrast to living a me-centered life, Jesus called for the exact opposite for His disciples (Matthew 20:25–27). Living a life of servanthood to God and others is living generously with all that one is, all that one has, and all that one does. It's a posture of the heart that aligns with Jesus.

A servant's heart is marked by compassion and prioritizing the needs of others. Servants are filled with humility, kindness, and a willingness to go the extra mile to help those in need.

When selfishness raises its ugly head, look around and see who you can bless. What do you have to share, what can you do, or who can you be that can make an impact in the lives of others?

He is the Lord, the Servant. Do you know Him?

ADDITIONAL SCRIPTURES ABOUT SERVING
MARK 9:35; JOHN 12:26; GALATIANS 5:13–14; 1 PETER 4:10

How do you cultivate a servant's heart?

____

____

____

____

What are some lessons to learn from Jesus as He laid down His title and served with a towel? (See John 13:1-17.)

____

____

____

____

Week 4 - Day 5

LORD, LET ME HAVE EYES TO SEE THOSE WHOM I CAN SERVE TODAY. EVERYTHING I DO FOR OTHERS, I DO FOR YOU. FORGIVE ME FOR MY SELFISHNESS AND GIVE ME A JOYFUL HEART TO BLESS OTHERS IN YOUR NAME.

AMEN.

WEEK FOUR
Group Discussion

The Bible tells us to love God and love people. When our vertical relationship is healthy, our horizontal relationships can improve. Discuss why this is true and when it might not be true.

____

____

____

____

The only person you can change is you. In friendship, a parent-child relationship, or marriage, how can you work on changing yourself?

____

____

____

____

What is your typical response to conflict—head in the sand or run to the battle? Discuss constructive ideas to remedy conflict.

Talk about what it means to "love your neighbor as yourself."

This week we discussed these names of God: my Peace, the God who sees me, my Strength, Servant. Share which name currently resonates with you the most and why.

WEEK
Five

Now may the God of peace
make you holy in every
way, and may your whole
spirit and soul
and body be kept
blameless until our Lord
Jesus Christ comes again.

1 Thessalonians 5:23

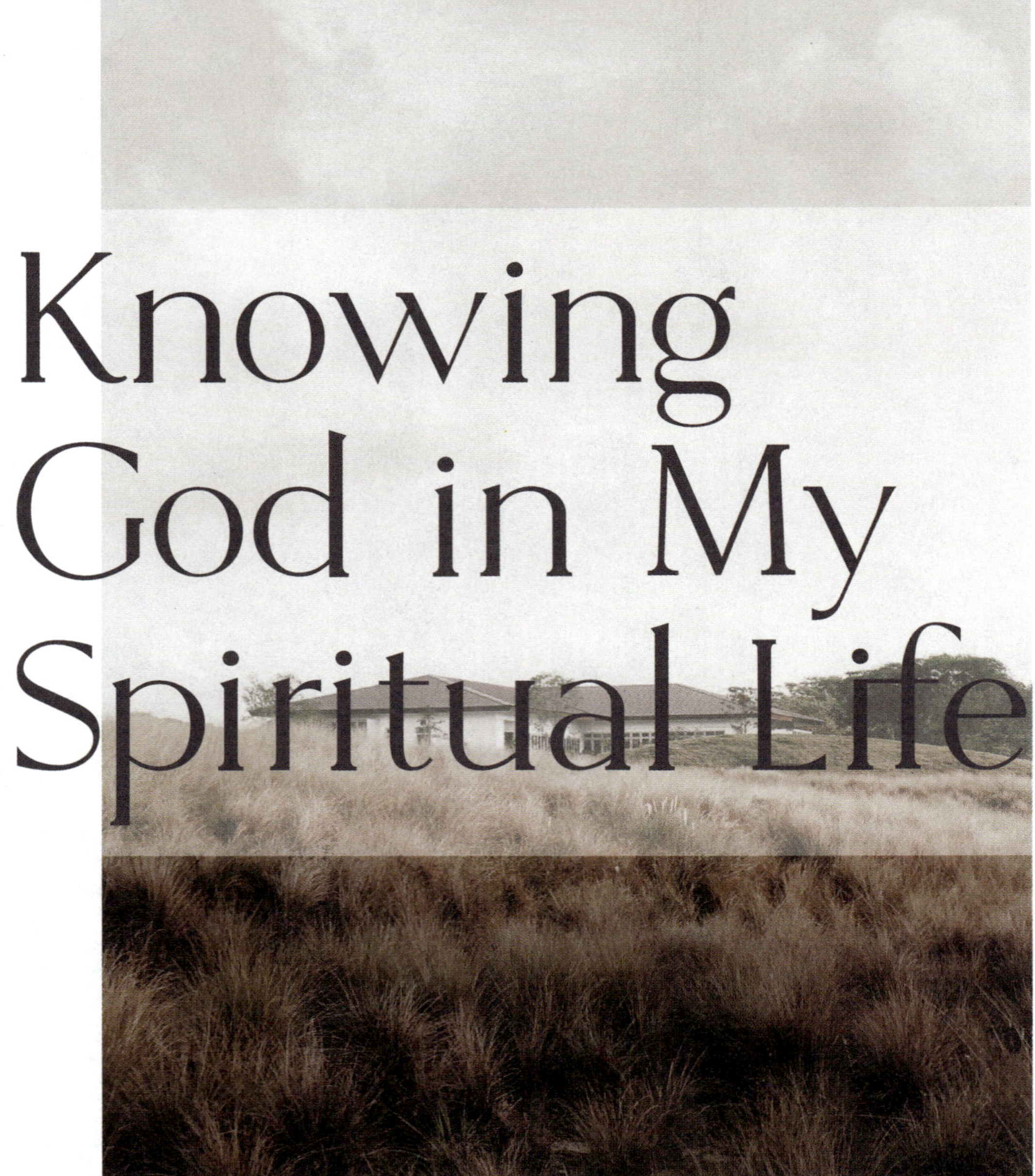

Knowing God in My Spiritual Life

Week 5 | Day 1

Knowing God in My Spiritual Life

God is a triune being, three in one: Father, Son and Holy Spirit. We are created in His image. We are a soul that has a spirit and lives in a physical body.

First Thessalonians 5:23 says it this way:

> NOW MAY THE GOD OF PEACE MAKE YOU HOLY IN EVERY WAY, AND MAY YOUR WHOLE SPIRIT AND SOUL AND BODY BE KEPT BLAMELESS UNTIL OUR LORD JESUS CHRIST COMES AGAIN.

When I invite Jesus into my heart to be Savior and Lord, I am born again! Hallelujah! Because God is Spirit, at this moment my spirit is awakened and becomes alive.

SOUL

BODY   SPIRIT

Our soul consists of our mind, will, and emotions. The importance of soul care is addressed frequently, but it spans beyond a vacation or spa day. We need a healthy soul since it is the place of decision-making.

Equally important, maintaining physical health is vital so that we don't sabotage our own potential and purpose. Just as caring for our physical body is critical to staying alive, it is the same with our spirit. We build up our spirit with spiritual disciplines, such as reading the Word, worship, prayer, and fasting.

And the part you feed and nurture the best is the one that will be strongest, becoming the primary decision-maker. Our soul is informed by our body (flesh), representing the things that are natural and carnal in nature. Our soul is informed by our spirit, that which connects and communicates with God.

This week we will look at some familiar aspects of our spiritual life and get acquainted with some correlating characteristics and names of God. Remember, we are learning the names of God, not for the sake of head knowledge, but to know Him more experientially and intimately.

Reflection

Which is stronger at this moment, your spirit or body? Make a list
of the strengths and weaknesses of each.

____

____

____

____

List the ways you are investing in your spiritual life and the benefits
you are experiencing. What is one thing you can work on this
week that will make a big difference?

____

____

____

____

Prayer

*LORD, I LAY MY SPIRITUAL LIFE AT YOUR FEET. HELP ME TO BUILD
GODLY CHARACTER AND PRACTICE DISCIPLINES THAT BRING ME
CLOSER TO YOU. AWAKEN MY SPIRIT TO KNOW YOU MORE.
THANK YOU FOR REVEALING YOURSELF TO ME THIS WEEK IN
WAYS I HAVE NEVER KNOWN BEFORE.*

AMEN.

When I Struggle to Forgive

Week 5 | Day 2

When I Struggle To Forgive

IN ALL YOUR WAYS ACKNOWLEDGE HIM, AND HE SHALL DIRECT YOUR PATHS.

PROVERBS 3:6 (NKJV)

IN ALL YOUR WAYS—WHEN YOUR WAY INCLUDES UNFORGIVENESS
KNOW—EXPERIENTIALLY, INTIMATELY KNOW THIS CHARACTERISTIC OF
HIM—THE LAMB OF GOD

Forgiveness is something that does not come naturally to us and is not always easy to do. When someone has done something grievous, our first thought is to do to them as they have done to us—an eye for an eye type of thing.

However, Jesus gave us a different way to respond. And it's not merely a suggestion.

"IF YOU FORGIVE THOSE WHO SIN AGAINST YOU, YOUR HEAVENLY FATHER WILL FORGIVE YOU. BUT IF YOU REFUSE TO FORGIVE OTHERS, YOUR FATHER WILL NOT FORGIVE YOUR SINS."

MATTHEW 6:14-15

We forgive because we have been forgiven—"just as God through Christ has forgiven you" (Ephesians 4:32). God forgives us through Christ for He is the "Lamb of God who takes away the sin of the world!" (John 1:29). Jesus became the Sinless Passover Lamb, willingly laying down His life for us. His sinless, holy life offered up the blood that became the final, once-for-all sacrifice. "It is finished!" (John 19:30).

This was the Father's plan all along, which Jesus obeyed every step of the way. His blood cleanses our sin, making us clean through and through. As we put our faith in Him, the "sacrifice that atones for our sins" (1 John 2:2), we obtain forgiveness from sin and our names are written in the Lamb's Book of Life (Revelation 21:27).

Forgiveness is a choice of the will, not of the emotions. It is a decision we consciously make according to the Word of God. It does not condone the offender's actions, nor is it an admission that the offense did not even happen. The alternative is to live with unforgiveness in our heart, which is a prison we create for ourself.

We are acquainted with the Lamb of God more intimately and personally when we are faced with the choice to forgive others. It is here that we can appreciate more fully the choice Jesus made to suffer and die for our sins.

Jesus coming as the Lamb did not show His weakness, but His obedience. When we forgive others, it is the same for us (Philippians 2:5–8).

He is the Lamb of God. Do you know Him?

ADDITIONAL SCRIPTURES ABOUT FORGIVENESS
ISAIAH 43:25; MATTHEW 18:21-22; ACTS 3:19; 1 JOHN 1:9

Reflection

What is the difference between forgiveness and condoning someone's behavior?

____

____

____

____

Are you harboring unforgiveness in your heart right now? Why is it important to live a life of foregiveness?

____

____

____

____

Prayer

LORD, BECAUSE YOU HAVE FORGIVEN ME, I FORGIVE
________________. EVEN WHEN I DON'T FEEL LIKE FORGIVING,
I MAKE THE CHOICE TO FORGIVE. CLEANSE ME FROM ALL
BITTERNESS OR ANY RESIDUE THAT WOULD LINGER IN MY HEART
AND AFFECT MY RELATIONSHIP WITH YOU. THANK YOU, JESUS,
FOR HELPING ME TO LET IT GO.

AMEN.

When I
Have Doubts

When I Have Doubts

IN ALL YOUR WAYS ACKNOWLEDGE HIM, AND HE SHALL DIRECT YOUR PATHS.

PROVERBS 3:6 (NKJV)

IN ALL YOUR WAYS—WHEN YOUR WAY INCLUDES DOUBT
KNOW—EXPERIENTIALLY, INTIMATELY KNOW THIS CHARACTERISTIC OF
HIM—I AM WHO I AM

Why is it on Sunday you can feel like God's woman of faith, but by Monday morning you can be doubting everything you believe?

The Bible has a few interesting stories about doubters. Jesus' disciple Thomas wins the prize by having the word attached to his name: Doubting Thomas (John 20:24–29). What about John the Baptist? He was the one who baptized Jesus, preparing the way for the Lord. He was even a relative of Jesus! But after being thrown in prison, he began doubting if Jesus was the Messiah. John sent word to Jesus to ask if he should wait for someone else (Matthew 11:2–6).

Moses was another infamous doubter, questioning God all along the way. When Moses asked God what His name was, He called himself, "I AM WHO I AM" (Exodus 3:14). He is the God who was, who is, and who will be.

Having doubts means that we are human, but it does not disqualify us from doing great things for God. What we do with our doubts is what matters. Doubt is different from unbelief: One is saying, "I question what I believe"; the other is saying, "I refuse to believe."

Bring your doubt to I AM WHO I AM. We don't need to feel embarrassment or shame, but simply come and present our uncertainty to God. He introduced himself to Moses as the God of his ancestors, Abraham, Isaac, and Jacob. He is the eternally existent One who is powerful enough to dispel doubts and infuse you with new faith and hope.

Instead of rehearsing your doubts, spend time rehearsing God's faithfulness to those in Scripture and stories from your own journey. Moses went from an insecure doubter to walking through the Red Sea. After that he sang:

When you are doubting God, remember that He is bigger than your problem and bigger than your doubts. The eternal God of the universe wants to walk with you through the unknown. So, doubt your doubts, believe your beliefs, and watch Him perform great wonders in front of you.

He is I AM WHO I AM. Do you know Him?

ADDITIONAL SCRIPTURES ABOUT DOUBT
PSALM 94:19; MATTHEW 21:21

Reflection

What are some topics in your life that bring up doubt?

____

____

____

____

What can you actively do to combat doubt?

____

____

____

____

Prayer

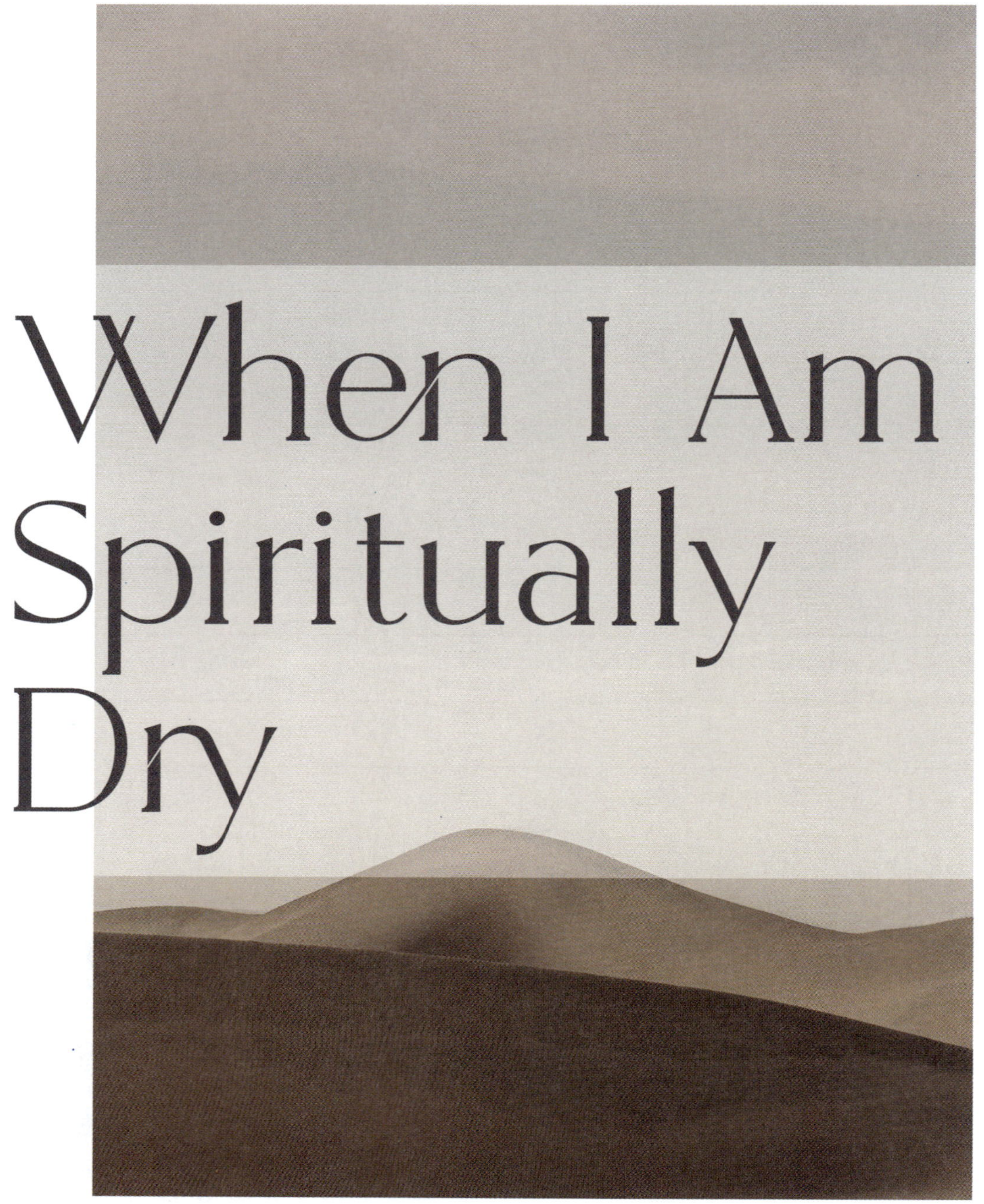

When I Am
Spiritually
Dry

Week 5 | Day 4

When I Am Spiritually Dry

IN ALL YOUR WAYS ACKNOWLEDGE HIM, AND HE SHALL DIRECT YOUR PATHS.

PROVERBS 3:6 (NKJV)

IN ALL YOUR WAYS—WHEN YOUR WAY INCLUDES SPIRITUAL DRYNESS
KNOW—EXPERIENTIALLY, INTIMATELY KNOW THIS CHARACTERISTIC OF
HIM—THE SOURCE OF LIVING WATER

Only a few animals, reptiles, and plants are designed to live in desert environments. Hot temperatures, dry air, and little water make for a challenging existence.

It is also challenging when walking through spiritually dry times. I can remember feeling alive, thriving in my relationship with Jesus and His Church. Bible reading and prayer were exciting portions of the day. Worshipping alone or in community was exhilarating. I sensed Him, felt His presence, and heard His voice.

Then silence. Like the turn of a spigot, the freshness evaporated—and my soul was dry.

There was a thirsty woman from Samaria who is known as the "woman at the well." She lived in a hot and arid place, disconnected from her community because of her unbecoming lifestyle. One day as she went to draw water from the well, she met Jesus—and everything changed. He told her,

> "ANYONE WHO DRINKS THIS WATER WILL SOON BECOME THIRSTY AGAIN. BUT THOSE WHO DRINK THE WATER I GIVE WILL NEVER BE THIRSTY AGAIN. IT BECOMES A FRESH, BUBBLING SPRING WITHIN THEM, GIVING THEM ETERNAL LIFE."
>
> JOHN 4:13-14

When your spirit feels bone-dry, what you need is the Living Water. Jesus will satiate and refresh your soul. Here's His invitation to you:

> "ANYONE WHO IS THIRSTY MAY COME TO ME! ANYONE WHO BELIEVES IN ME MAY COME AND DRINK! FOR THE SCRIPTURES DECLARE, 'RIVERS OF LIVING WATER WILL FLOW FROM HIS HEART.'"
>
> JOHN 7:37-38

In this passage, the verb tense of the word *drink* is the present imperative. It implies a repeated, continuous action. Make it your habit to frequently, liberally, and lavishly drink of the Living Water. See how you flourish!

He is Living Water. Do you know Him?

ADDITIONAL SCRIPTURES ABOUT SPIRITUAL DRYNESS
PSALM 63:1; JEREMIAH 29:13; MATTHEW 5:6; REVELATION 22:17

During a spiritually dry season, what does drinking Living Water look like?

____

____

____

____

Water is necessary for life. How is the Living Water necessary for our daily life?

____

____

____

Prayer

LORD, WHEN MY CUP IS EMPTY, FILL ME UP TO OVERFLOWING.
POUR YOUR LIVING WATER INTO MY DRY AND WEARY SOUL.
DEEPEN THE WELL OF MY SOUL TO WANT MORE OF YOU.

AMEN.

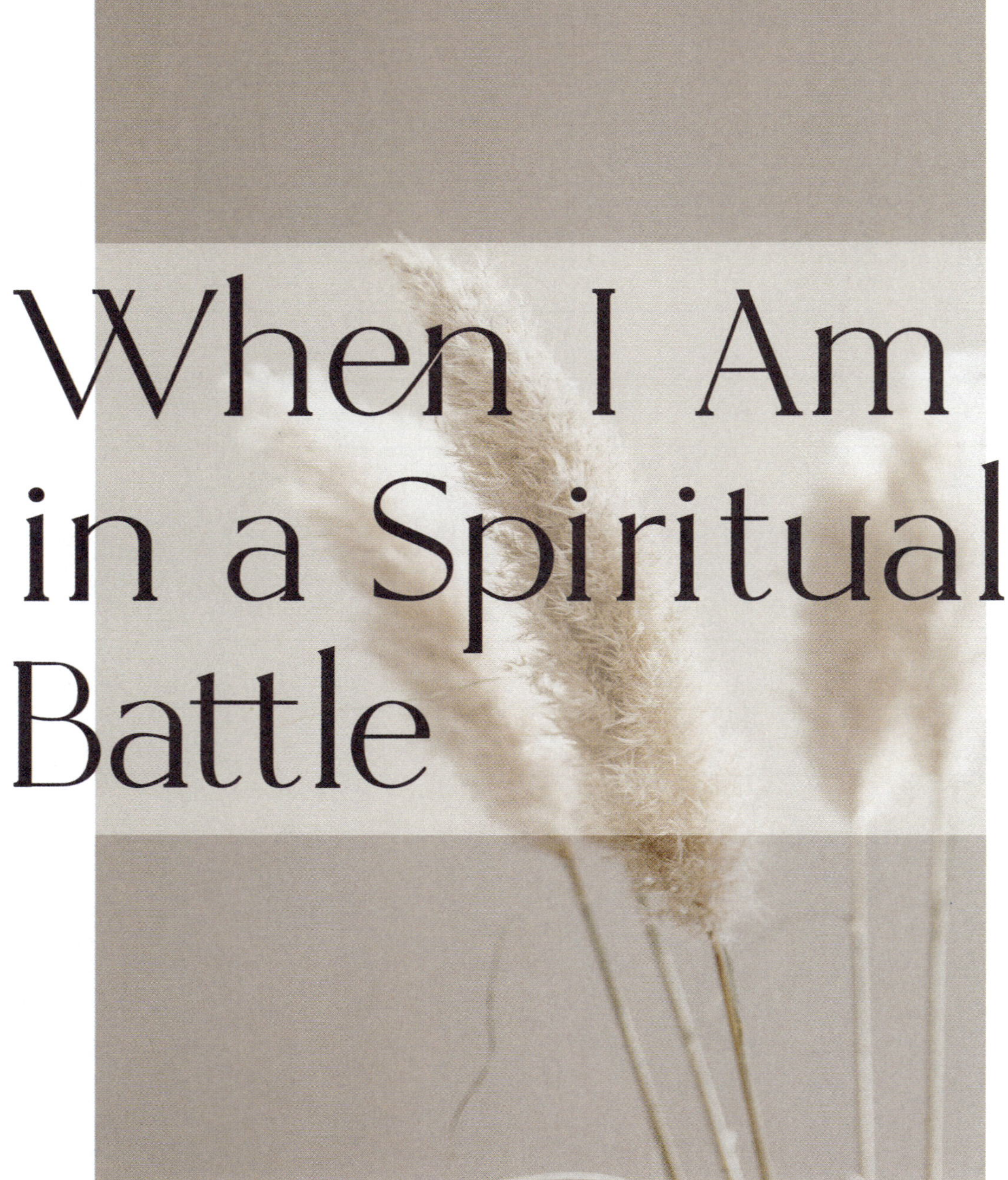

When I Am in a Spiritual Battle

Week 5 | Day 5

When I Am in a Spiritual Battle

IN ALL YOUR WAYS ACKNOWLEDGE HIM, AND HE SHALL DIRECT YOUR PATHS.

PROVERBS 3:6 (NKJV)

IN ALL YOUR WAYS—WHEN YOUR WAY INCLUDES SPIRITUAL BATTLES
KNOW—EXPERIENTIALLY, INTIMATELY KNOW THIS CHARACTERISTIC OF
HIM—THE COMMANDER OF THE LORD'S ARMY

War has existed for nearly as long as humans have inhabited the earth. Age after age, humankind battles for power and domination, to subdue their enemies and gain their possessions.

As Joshua and the Children of Israel crossed the Jordan River and entered the Promised Land, they also entered a time of warfare. Canaan was filled with milk and honey, but also with the enemies of Israel.

The Lord prepared them for the battles ahead. Jericho was first. It was a fortified city, with walls that stood forty-six feet above ground level and were seemingly impenetrable.

The Israelites had just come out of forty years in the wilderness. In the natural, they were ill-prepared to defeat this well-fortified city. But a man with a sword came to Joshua (Joshua 5:13) and introduced himself:

"I AM THE COMMANDER OF THE LORD'S ARMY."

JOSHUA 5:14

God gave Joshua the strategy for that battle. The Israelites were to march around Jericho one time every day for six days. On the seventh day they were to march about the city six times in silence, and on the seventh lap they were to raise their voices. It wasn't really about what they did, it was about their obedience to what God had said.

As believers, we are also in a war. A spiritual battle is raging around us in the unseen realm, a battle that we wage on our knees.

> WE ARE HUMAN, BUT WE DON'T WAGE WAR AS HUMANS DO. WE USE GOD'S MIGHTY WEAPONS, NOT WORLDLY WEAPONS, TO KNOCK DOWN THE STRONGHOLDS OF HUMAN REASONING AND TO DESTROY FALSE ARGUMENTS.
>
> 2 CORINTHIANS 10:3-4

When we are in the midst of a raging battle, remember God sent "a man," possibly God himself came to Joshua identified as the Commander of the heavenly armies. He gave his "rank" and introduced a winning strategy to defeat the enemies of God's people.

We have spiritual weapons that knock down strongholds and thwart the enemy. These weapons include God's Word, intercessory prayer, fasting, and worship. We also incorporate trust, obedience, and God's timing. We put on the full armor of God (Ephesians 6:10–18) and listen to our Commander as He gives the orders (Acts 13:2; 16:6–10).

He is the Commander. Do you know Him?

ADDITIONAL SCRIPTURES ABOUT SPIRITUAL WARFARE
JOHN 10:10; COLOSSIANS 1:13-14; 1 PETER 5:8-9

Reflection

What are some spiritual weapons with which you can fight the enemy?

____

____

____

____

Spiritual battles require different strategies. You need to be baptized in the Holy Spirit. Ask Jesus to fill you now with the Holy Spirit.

____

____

____

____

Prayer

LORD, YOU HAVE PUT THE HIGH PRAISES OF GOD IN MY MOUTH AND A TWO-EDGED SWORD (THE WORD) IN MY HAND (PSALM 149:6). I AM STRONG IN THE LORD AND THE POWER OF HIS MIGHT AS I PUT ON THE FULL ARMOR OF GOD (EPHESIANS 6:10). THANK YOU FOR YOUR PROTECTION IN THE BATTLE AND THE VICTORY YOU WILL BRING.

AMEN.

The physical realm is seen, and the spiritual realm is unseen. How can you measure your spiritual growth and maturity when you cannot see it?

____

____

____

____

Who is the Holy Spirit and how does His job description differ from the roles of the Father and the Son?

____

____

____

____

Have you been baptized in the Holy Spirit? (Acts 2:1–4) Take some time to
pray with each other so you will be filled.

____

____

____

____

You are in a spiritual battle. Discuss what spiritual weapons you have to
fight the enemy.

____

____

____

____

This week we discussed these names of God: the Lamb of God, I AM
WHO I AM, the source of Living Water, the Commander. Share which
name currently resonates with you the most and why.

____

____

____

____

WEEK
Six

"You must love the LORD your God with all your heart, all your soul, and all your mind."

Matthew 22:37

Knowing God in My Intellectual Life

Week 6 | Day 1

Knowing God in My Intellectual Life

As human beings, we have a remarkable intellectual capacity that sets us apart from animals. Our ability to think, reason, learn, and communicate is possible as our brain connects, communicates, and processes with its billions of neurons.

Faith in God does not mean that we throw out reason, check our brain at the door, and blindly follow. In fact, the Lord invites us to engage with Him and love Him with our whole being.

JESUS REPLIED, "YOU MUST LOVE THE LORD YOUR GOD WITH ALL YOUR HEART, ALL YOUR SOUL, AND ALL YOUR MIND."

MATTHEW 22:37

Jesus can handle our tough questions. He gave us minds that analyze, observe, perceive, and imagine. We are fearfully and wonderfully made by our Creator (Psalm 139:14). Engaging in robust study, inquiring about spiritual matters, and examining our theology only enriches our faith. In fact, curious and inquisitive people usually learn the most!

Remember to remain teachable and humble. The Holy Spirit can challenge our thinking, traditions, and practices, so stay nimble as you learn and grow. Make sure to have trusted spiritual leaders with whom you can process.

Maturing as disciples of Jesus means stretching our mind and challenging our thoughts. Being students of the Word means that we are always in the school of the Holy Spirit, increasing in spiritual wisdom and understanding.

This week invite the Lord into your intellectual life. Become aware of your thoughts and every default setting in your mind that is not healthy or beneficial. Remember, you are learning the names of God not for the sake of head knowledge, but to know Him more experientially and intimately.

Make a list of spiritual topics you have questions about or have yet to understand. How can you increase your knowledge on these subjects? Work on one this week.

____

____

____

____

When your brain is working overtime, what do you do to slow down and process with the Lord?

____

____

____

____

Prayer

LORD, I LAY MY INTELLECTUAL LIFE AT YOUR FEET. THANK YOU FOR THE MIND YOU GAVE ME. HELP ME TO KNOW YOU MORE WITH EVERY PART OF MY THINKING, REASONING, AND LEARNING. MAY I GROW IN THE GRACE AND KNOWLEDGE OF YOU EVERY DAY. THANK YOU FOR REVEALING YOURSELF TO ME THIS WEEK IN WAYS I HAVE NEVER KNOWN BEFORE.

AMEN.

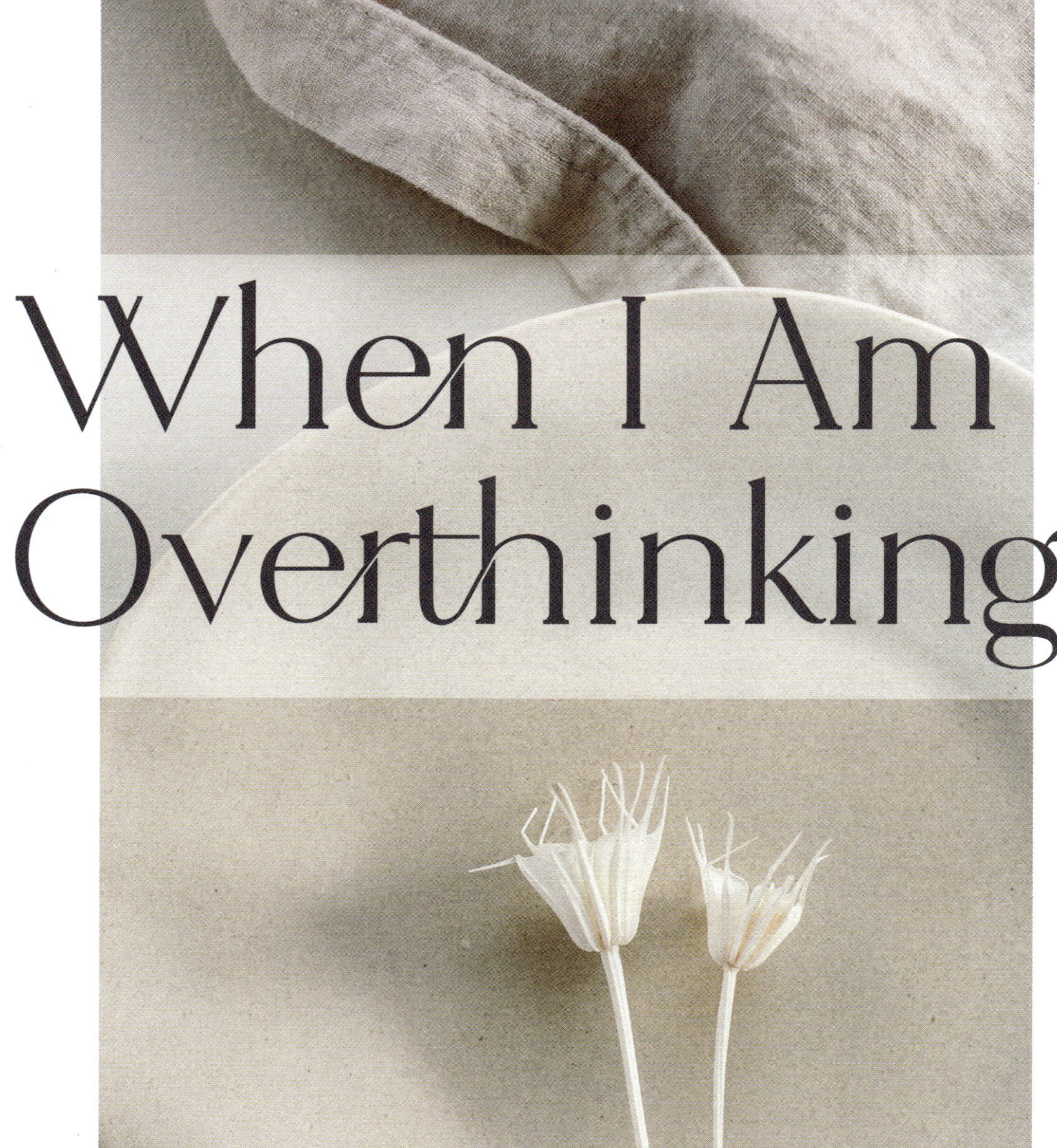

When I Am Overthinking

Week 6 | Day 2

When I Am Overthinking

IN ALL YOUR WAYS ACKNOWLEDGE HIM, AND HE SHALL DIRECT YOUR PATHS.

PROVERBS 3:6 (NKJV)

IN ALL YOUR WAYS—WHEN YOUR WAY INCLUDES OVERTHINKING
KNOW—EXPERIENTIALLY, INTIMATELY KNOW THIS CHARACTERISTIC OF
HIM—CHRIST, THE WISDOM OF GOD

Think! Think! Think! Surely, we can figure it out!

Our minds are the activity center of contemplation, thought, and reflection that helps us navigate life. Our intellect helps shape our beliefs, reach decisions, and choose preferences. Thinking is the process that moves us in a desired trajectory. Author Mark Batterson, encourages us to "dream big, think long, pray hard" as we follow God's path for our life.[4]

Thinking through a matter is smart. We incorporate analytical thinking, critical thinking, and creative thinking in everyday life. But when we overthink, we tend to ruminate on negative thoughts, worries, and fears, which often leads to anxiety and stress. It can also lead to decision paralysis, where we become indecisive and unable to make choices due to our over-analyzing and second-guessing.

[4]Mark Batterson, *The Circle Maker: Praying Circles around Your Biggest Dreams and Greatest Fears* (Grand Rapids, MI: Zondervan, 2011), 151.

In the Book of James, we learn about different kinds of wisdom (James 3:13–18). Human wisdom has its place and is important, but it has limitations, even at its best. Then there is "wisdom from above" (verse 17), which is characterized by purity, gentleness, humility, mercy, good deeds, and sincerity.

Proverbs 3:5 (NKJV) instructs us this way:

> TRUST IN THE LORD WITH ALL YOUR HEART; DO NOT DEPEND ON YOUR OWN UNDERSTANDING.

When we are in the spin cycle of thoughts and cannot find a way out, call out to Christ, who is the wisdom of God.

> CHRIST IS THE POWER OF GOD AND THE WISDOM OF GOD.
>
> 1 CORINTHIANS 1:24

Knowing Christ is knowing wisdom up close and personal. It is more than acquiring a quality that we need, but it is knowing, interacting with, and conversing with the Person who is wisdom, Christ.

We have our part to do to acquire wisdom, knowledge, and understanding (Proverbs 2:1–6). And we connect with Christ, the wisdom of God. Listening is required here. Silently sit in His presence. Quiet your heart and mind to be still and attentive to the Holy Spirit. He will speak!

He is Christ, the wisdom of God. Do you know Him?

ADDITIONAL SCRIPTURES ABOUT DEALING WITH THOUGHTS
PSALM 94:8-11; PROVERBS 16:9; COLOSSIANS 3:1-2; 1 PETER 1:13

James 1:5 says that when we need wisdom, we just need to ask for it. What are some areas in which you need the wisdom of God to speak?

____

____

____

____

How is godly wisdom different from earthly wisdom? (See James 3:13–17.)

____

____

____

____

Prayer

LORD, I NEED WISDOM. I KNOW THAT YOU DON'T JUST HAVE WISDOM, BUT YOUR VERY NATURE IS WISDOM. AS I KNOW YOU MORE, WOULD YOU INCREASE AND REVEAL YOUR WISDOM IN MY LIFE? THANK YOU, LORD, I'M LISTENING.

AMEN.

When I
Struggle
with Control

Week 6 | Day 3

When I Struggle with Control

IN ALL YOUR WAYS ACKNOWLEDGE HIM, AND HE SHALL DIRECT YOUR PATHS.

PROVERBS 3:6 (NKJV)

IN ALL YOUR WAYS—WHEN YOUR WAY INCLUDES CONTROL
KNOW—EXPERIENTIALLY, INTIMATELY KNOW THIS CHARACTERISTIC OF
HIM—THE LORD

"Jesus, I am Yours!" We sing it in songs of worship and talk about it as a desire of our hearts, but surrendering ourself to Jesus is not a one-time event. Our human nature battles for control as our will does a tug-of-war with His will. We faithfully pray, "Your Kingdom come," but we also need to include, "My kingdom go."

Feeling out of control or the feeling of being controlled can be like free-falling out of an airplane. When life is threatened by disruption that is outside our control, our will naturally kicks in to take charge.

Control is a lordship issue that determines who is calling the shots in our life. The commitment to Jesus' lordship involves surrendering our will and desires to Him, submitting to His authority, and seeking to obey His commands. It is a lifelong journey of growing in faith and allowing Jesus to transform every area of our life. He wants this of us:

> IF YOU OPENLY DECLARE THAT JESUS IS LORD AND BELIEVE IN YOUR HEART THAT GOD RAISED HIM FROM THE DEAD, YOU WILL BE SAVED.
>
> ROMANS 10:9

The invitation is for Jesus to be both Savior and Lord. To confess Him as Savior means that I believe salvation is a free gift from God because of Jesus' sacrifice. To confess Jesus as Lord means that I believe He is the Son of God, the Savior of humanity, and the ultimate authority over all creation.

When life is chaotic, instead of instinctively grabbing tightly to everything or everyone, call out to the Lord. Submit to His plans, His ways, and His timing. Lift your hands as a sign of surrender and worship the Lord your God. He is Lord of heaven and earth. He is Lord of lords. He is the Lord of the heavenly hosts. He is Lord of all. Is He the Lord of your life?

He is Jesus Christ, the Lord. Do you know Him?

ADDITIONAL SCRIPTURES ABOUT SURRENDER
PSALM 37:7; MATTHEW 16:24; ROMANS 12:1; JAMES 4:7

Reflection

What area in your heart is a constant battle for control?

____

____

____

____

Remembering what God has done for you in the past is a reminder of His faithfulness and trustworthiness. Make a list of the things He has done for you. How does this make a difference in the area of His lordship in your life?

____

____

____

____

Prayer

THANK YOU, LORD, FOR YOUR GOODNESS AND FAITHFULNESS
TO ME. I KNOW YOU KNIT ME TOGETHER IN MY
MOTHER'S WOMB AND KNOW WHAT IS BEST FOR ME.
THANK YOU FOR BEING LORD OF MY LIFE.

AMEN.

When Life
Is Not Logical

Week 6 | Day 4

When Life Is Not Logical

IN ALL YOUR WAYS ACKNOWLEDGE HIM, AND HE SHALL DIRECT YOUR PATHS.

PROVERBS 3:6 (NKJV)

IN ALL YOUR WAYS—WHEN YOUR WAY IS NOT LOGICAL
KNOW—EXPERIENTIALLY, INTIMATELY KNOW THIS CHARACTERISTIC OF
HIM—THE MOST HIGH, *ELYON*

Thank God for our incredible minds! We have the ability to access reason, deduction, sound judgment, and even common sense to make decisions.

Sometimes though, life does not make any rational sense—an accident, a mistake, or a misunderstanding happens. Even when we have done the right things, planned properly, and used wisdom, an unforeseen left turn out of nowhere occasionally happens to everyone. We can't figure it out. We desperately desire clarity and resolution. We want to scream, "Let me tie it up with a nice bow and move on where my astute capabilities will serve me once again."

The great and prosperous King Nebuchadnezzar of Babylon had bad dreams and sought out all the wise men of the kingdom for the interpretation. None could deliver, until Daniel, a Hebrew taken captive who was serving in the palace, was brought before the king and heard his dream.

"Most High" is a title of God that Daniel intentionally used when he addressed King Nebuchadnezzar. He acknowledged the king's earthy position and authority, while also using language for the king to know that there is another who is higher than he.

When life's circumstances defy logic, this is the time you get to know the Most High God. This name characterizes His greatness and explains that there is no one above, no one higher, and no one greater than Him.

We can find comfort knowing that our Most High God is above everything.

Isaiah recorded:

God is above human logic and understanding—including your limited understanding. Invite the Most High into your dilemma and ask Him to enlighten your thinking to know His thoughts, His ways, and His wisdom.

He is the Most High God. Do you know Him?

ADDITIONAL SCRIPTURES ABOUT HUMAN LOGIC AND GOD'S THOUGHTS
NUMBERS 23:19; ISAIAH 40:28; ROMANS 11:33; 1 CORINTHIANS 2:16

Reflection

Identify any issues in your life that don't make sense.

____

____

____

____

What is the benefit of being in relationship with the Most High God?

____

____

____

____

Prayer

LORD, WHEN I DON'T UNDERSTAND, I LOOK TO YOU. WHEN SOMETHING IS TRYING TO ELEVATE ITSELF IN MY LIFE, I REMEMBER THAT YOU ARE MOST HIGH, AND I GIVE YOU THIS PLACE IN MY LIFE. I TRUST THAT YOU KNOW THE WAY AND YOU WILL SHOW ME THE WAY.

AMEN.

When I'm Troubled by Past Memories

Week 6 | Day 5

When I'm Troubled by Past Memories

IN ALL YOUR WAYS ACKNOWLEDGE HIM, AND HE SHALL DIRECT YOUR PATHS.

PROVERBS 3:6 (NKJV)

IN ALL YOUR WAYS—WHEN YOUR WAY HAS INESCAPABLE MEMORIES
KNOW—EXPERIENTIALLY, INTIMATELY KNOW THIS CHARACTERISTIC OF
HIM—THE REDEEMER

Human memory is a cognitive function of the brain where information is stored and retrieved. Memory can include past events or the ability to remember general information and facts.

Painful memories can feel as though they happened yesterday, even when they occurred years before. They can be a constant, present state of mind, haunted by the repeated replaying of events that keep it an open and festering wound.

Accidents that occur in nature can be extremely treacherous. Victims may need extraction from a vehicle, mountain terrain, or a water rescue. Aircraft might be needed when the victims are inaccessible by foot. This requires the expertise of emergency search and rescue teams. Their goal is first to rescue, and if necessary to recover. Rescue is for the living and recovery is for the presumed dead.

Similar to a search and rescue team, Jesus seeks to rescue us from the penalty of sin and death. And He went even further to recover what has been lost. From the ruins of our life, He redeems the ashes of anguish and gives a crown of beauty. He takes our sorrow and grief, exchanging it for joy. We give Him our despair and He gives us the ability to praise (Isaiah 61:3).

> "HE IS YOUR REDEEMER, THE HOLY ONE OF ISRAEL, THE GOD OF ALL THE EARTH."
>
> ISAIAH 54:5

Redeem means to pay a price in order to secure the release of something or someone. The Lord loves us so much that He paid the ransom for us to be healed and restored. He has the ability to both forgive our past sins and mend our wounds.

What He said to the Israelites, He says to you as one of His children:

> "DO NOT BE AFRAID, FOR I HAVE RANSOMED YOU. I HAVE CALLED YOU BY NAME; YOU ARE MINE."
>
> ISAIAH 43:1

Instead of staying in misery, call on your Redeemer. Trust Him with your memories and pain. Stay close to your Redeemer and watch Him put the pieces back together.

He is your Redeemer. Do you know Him?

ADDITIONAL SCRIPTURE ABOUT PAST MEMORIES
PSALMS 32:1-5; 62:8; PHILIPPIANS 3:12-14; 4:8-9

Reflection

Painful memories can keep you stuck in the past. Is there an area of past pain that keeps you from moving forward?

____

____

____

____

What would freedom from that past pain look like?

____

____

____

____

Prayer

LORD, AS I SIT QUIETLY IN YOUR PRESENCE, I ASK YOU TO TAKE THE THINGS THAT ARE BROKEN IN ME AND MAKE THEM WHOLE. I BELIEVE YOU ARE TAKING WHAT THE ENEMY MEANT FOR EVIL AND TURNING IT FOR GOOD (GENESIS 50:20).

AMEN.

The Lord can handle your tough questions. Share some of your unanswered questions and what you can do, if anything, to find an answer.

____

____

____

____

What are ways that you can love the Lord with your mind and intellect?

____

____

____

____

When painful memories and doubts swirl in your mind, it can be challenging to trust the Lord. How do you guard your heart from cynicism and instead build up your faith?

____

____

____

____

In the psalms, Kind David confessed, "I will rejoice" (Psalm 118:24), and "I will sing" (Psalm 89:1). When is willpower effective? When is it not?

____

____

____

____

This week, we discussed these names of God: Wisdom of God, the Lord, the Most High, my Redeemer. Share which name currently resonates with you the most and why.

____

____

____

____

Conclusion

Knowing God more intimately is a lifetime pursuit. I pray that sweet times of communion with Him will ruin us of being content with anything this world has to offer. He meets with us in different ways and oftentimes He even surprises us:

- In powerful times of corporate worship
- While appreciating the magnificence of nature
- Laying prostrate before His presence
- In our tears
- In dancing and celebration
- In His Word
- In prayer and intercession

What a privilege to know the love of the Father, the sacrifice of Jesus, and the comfort of the Holy Spirit.

May we be *captivated* by His presence all the days of our life.

"BUT THE PEOPLE WHO KNOW THEIR GOD SHALL BE STRONG, AND CARRY OUT GREAT EXPLOITS"

DANIEL 11:32 (NKJV)